Is

D0430643

Is It Addiction?

IS IT
LOVE
or
IS IT
ADDICTION?

BRENDA
SCHAEFFER

SECOND EDITION

HAZELDEN®

Hazelden
Center City, Minnesota 55012-0176
1-800-328-0094
1-651-213-4590(Fax)
http://www.hazelden.org

Library of Congress Cataloging-in-Publication Data
Schaeffer, Brenda.
    Is it love or is it addiction? / Brenda Schaeffer.
        p.   cm.
    Includes bibliographical references and index.
    ISBN 1-56838-140-9
    1. Relationship addiction.   2. Love.   I. Title.
RC552.R44S34   1997
158.2—DC21   97-27921
                                                        CIP

        06   05   04   11   10   9

Book design by Will H. Powers
Typesetting by Stanton Publication Services, Inc.
Cover design by David Spohn

The vignettes in this book are composites of actual situations and persons, although some story lines in the vignettes have been created by the author for illustrative purposes. The autobiographical sketches are real, although the names have been changed. Any resemblance to specific persons, living or dead, or specific events, is entirely coincidental.

For my children, Heidi and Gordy, that they may know healthy love; for my late father, Ralph Furtman, in gratitude for his steadfast support and caring; for my late mother, Bernice Furtman, in acknowledgment of her permission to be all that I can be. May the souls of my parents know a peace they so deserve.

A good book is a supple and yielding thing. It is meant to be argued with, challenged, marked up. It is a battle ground for ideas and should show some evidence of a fight or at least some preliminary skirmishes. It is good for igniting minds. It is not the be-all and end-all of a balanced and productive life, but it can touch off needed thoughts and action.

NORMAN COUSINS, Human Options

Contents

Acknowledgments

A book begins as a creative thought in its author's mind. The road from idea to publication is a long and sometimes arduous one. My road contained many supportive people whom I wish to gratefully acknowledge. I wish to thank Muriel James, Jean Clarke, and Patricia Daoust for encouraging me to write; my brother, Michael Furtman; my friends Dr. Bart Knapp and Lynnell Mickelsen for their critical review of the first draft. Their honesty and encouragement are deeply appreciated. I wish to thank Pam Miller for her creative editing. Nancy Barrett, my typist, deserves special thanks for miraculously transposing my handwritten words into legible type. Thanks, also, to my agent, Vicky Lansky, for her enthusiastic support of my manuscript, and to my secretary, Jan Johannes, for working odd hours to meet deadlines.

I wish to extend grateful appreciation to those at Hazelden Educational Materials who believed in and encouraged the publishing of the first edition of this book—Jim Heaslip, Beth Milligan, and Pat Benson. Thanks, too, to editors Judy Delaney and Brian Lynch, who took the time to care about my perceptions and feelings.

I am, perhaps, most grateful to the clients who took the time to live and validate the theory I write about, especially those who wrote their stories so others can experience hope.

Thanks to Rev. Fred W. Hutchinson for his spiritual guidance and support. A very special thank you to my children, Heidi and Gordy, for their loving acceptance of me and the time it took to write this book.

And to Ted, a special thank you for the opportunity to live the circle of love and friendship in ways that helped me grow.

In this second edition, I would be remiss if I did not mention those who have been so important to me the past ten years and to those who contributed their thoughts to this revision. Heartfelt thanks go to: Arapata McKay, Peter R. Richards, Patrick Carnes, Jennifer Schneider, Sally Stevens, Christina Storbeck, Mark Laaser, Helen Palmer, Jacquelyn Small, Bart Knapp, Homer Mittelstadt, Barry McKee, Jerry Buckanaga, Linda Piscitelli Wolf. Special thanks go to Hazelden editors Steve Lehman and Dan Odegard, who understand the importance of the written word.

The following publishers have generously given permission to use quotations from copyrighted works: From *The Prophet,* by Kahlil Gibran, copyright 1923, renewed 1951 by Administrators C.T.A. of Kahlil Gibran Estate, and Mary G. Gibran. Reprinted with permission of Alfred A. Knopf. From *Scripts People Live: Transactional Analysis of Life Scripts* by Claude Steiner, copyright 1974. Reprinted with permission of the author. From *The Bridge Across Forever: A True Love Story* by Richard Bach, copyright 1984. Reprinted with permission of the author. From *Human Options* by Norman Cousins, copyright 1981. Used with permission of W. W. Norton and Company, Inc. From *The Velveteen Rabbit* by Margery Williams, copyright 1975. Reprinted with permission of Doubleday. From *Love and Addiction* by Stanton Beele, copyright 1975. Reprinted with permission of Taplinger Publishing. From *The Art of Loving* by Erich Fromm, copyright 1956. Reprinted with permission of Harper and Row. From *The Sex Contract* by Helen E. Fisher, copyright 1982. Reprinted with permission of William Morrow and Company.

Preface

It has been ten years since the first publication of *Is It Love or Is It Addiction?* Its phenomenal success was a gift in many ways. It provided me with the opportunity to speak to an international audience. It allowed me to hear relationship stories from many people of diverse cultural backgrounds. Mostly, it confirmed that what I had written about is a universal theme. People everywhere are struggling to have more meaningful relationships. I have met men struggling to change those cultural habits that shame them for being vulnerable, or tell them it is healthy and macho to act in sexually addictive ways. I have met women struggling to call attention to our cultural endorsement of unhealthy dependencies and romantic illusions. Everywhere, I have met women and men confused about what is healthy, mature, interdependent love and what is compulsive, dependent, addictive, immature love. I have been reminded how many people hold back their love because of being wounded by a parent, friend, partner, society, or cultural group. People both desperately want and yet fear intimate relationships. The result is loneliness, isolation, pain, violence, and more betrayal.

So, is it love, or is it addiction? The answer is that it is probably a little of both. In that regard, this book is for anyone wanting to improve important love relationships, whether they are with children, parents, friends, peers, siblings, partners, or lovers. In my frame of reference, *love addiction* is an inclusive term in that it includes men and women, both heterosexual and homosexual, who have been referred to as "addicts" and "co-addicts," "codependents," and "love avoidant." It is for the single and the coupled. Love addiction may or may not include a romantic high or sexual addiction.

Sometimes love feels good and sometimes it feels bad. Often a person does not understand why. In spite of the proliferation of self-help books on the subject, love relationships remain a profound mystery. Why do we have certain attractions? Why do we continue to want relationships even after a devastating loss? What is it about a relationship that is so powerful that we fear commitment? Am I staying in a relationship for the right or wrong reason? Why is transforming our love life so important? Am I in love or in addiction? These questions are universal and deserve answers.

As a psychotherapist, I'm asked to help others ease their emotional pain. I'm reminded over and over again how basic is the need for love. In spite of the bereavement we feel when a loved one dies or a relationship ends, we seem determined to keep loving. Why? Is it because we are compelled to fill some mysterious inner need? Are we using it to avoid the bombardment of stress that contemporary life produces? Are we responding to a deeper need to connect soul-to-soul? Or is it because we believe at some level that true, deep love is the only constant we can count on in this somewhat perilous life?

The problems in love relationships stem not from the nature of love. True love is life-giving. It is an expansive, nourishing energy that knows no limits. It does not injure, it heals. Problems arise from the fear that originates in a violation of trust. Such violations make it difficult to be vulnerable to love again. In the wake of such violations we become guarded. The result is relationships that have more drama than intimacy.

Being in a relationship that is floundering can be like having a pain in the neck or an aggravating headache. And, when we are sick, we lose ourselves. Our capacity for creative living gets sapped as we instead focus on our pain. We become driven to find relief from that pain, seeking quick fixes in the form of substances, people, and processes outside of ourselves. Obsessive illnesses and addictions often result. When the attachment is to a person, it can become a love addiction.

We live in a unique period of time, one fraught with contradictions. Many people seek a life of wellness. Many feel the soul's yearning for a deeper level of living. There is an explosion of knowledge on addiction, love relationships, and self-help. Yet we hear in the

news that when a twenty-four-year-old woman ends an abusive relationship with her twenty-nine-year-old boyfriend, she is murdered,
shot in the face, and her family fears for their lives. The Secretary of
Defense acknowledges that 61 percent of women in the military have
been sexually harassed. Incidents of domestic violence seem to be on
the increase. How is it that as a culture we are simultaneously seeking
wellness and descending into a well of violence?

The fields of addiction treatment and mental health care are
under attack from the media and cultural critics and from within
their own ranks. The addiction model has been too broadly applied,
some claim, and has thereby lost its usefulness as a tool for understanding and treating human dysfunction. The idea of the inner
child as a metaphor with profound therapeutic value becomes fod-
der for stand-up comedians and the vitriol of talk radio. Victims of
abuse are told their memories are fantasies. Our society continues to
expend far more money on feeding and expanding our addictions
than it spends on treating them. While there is concern for treating
the victims of sexual abuse, we continue to let the perpetrators go
untreated. Professionals in various fields still argue whether an addiction is a sin, a crime, or a disease. Some addiction specialists question whether a process, such as sex or love relationships (as opposed
to a substance, such as cocaine or nicotine), can be addicting at all.

It is time to stop arguing about our meaning and methods. The
reality is that we have a problem of massive proportions that requires
all of us to transcend our fears and differences. We must all help
transform a world that is crying out for knowledge of a healthier way
of living.

The events of the past ten years have only served to reinforce what
I wrote in the first edition of this book. Almost everyone has addictive tendencies. We know that we can become addicted to alcohol
and other drugs and that we have excellent programs to treat those
addictions. There are other addictions that can hamper our lives as
well, but they are not always recognized or addressed. This list includes food, exercise, consumerism, religious cults, spiritual highs,
nicotine, sugar, caffeine, sex, gambling, work, computers, television,
parenting, love objects, romance, pain, and illness. Perhaps you

recognize an obsession of your own among them. If you do, be kind to yourself. We live in a world that provides hundreds more experiences than our parents had. We are constantly bombarded with more information than we can possibly take in and process. We have more demands on our time. We hear threatening news each day. And in the midst of this we are expected to live our love relationships well, if not perfectly. I used to say that life is like a thousand-piece puzzle and we are lucky if we have 30 percent of the pieces. Now, with the barrage of information, images, and ideas we encounter daily, that percentage is going down.

The focus of this book is to foster an understanding of love addiction—what it is and is not, how to identify it, and even more important, how to get out of it. It is intended to be a hopeful book that helps you identify the characteristics of healthy love and frees you to live life more abundantly. As you will learn, real love is not addiction, nor is addiction love. Yet, because of the human condition, these two experiences can come together and result in tremendous pain and suffering. We must be wise in the ways we express love. My hope is that you will find at least one piece of wisdom here that impacts your love life in a meaningful way. This book is not intended to cure specific problems. However, with increased awareness, we can begin to solve relationship problems with more compassion and with lasting effect.

My hope is that this book gives you a few more pieces to life's puzzle.

I

The Reality of Addictive Love

1

The Power of Love

Healthy Love

In *The Art of Loving,* Erich Fromm, the German-born American psychoanalyst, says most efforts to love fail unless a person has actively tried to develop his or her *individual* potential and personality. Fromm defines love as "the expression of productiveness [which] implies care, respect, responsibility, and knowledge; a striving towards growth and happiness of the loved person, rooted in one's own capacity to love." Concepts we often associate with healthy human loving include affection, caring, valuing, trust, acceptance, giving, joy, and vulnerability. Love is a state of being that emanates from within us and extends outward. It is energy, it is unconditional, it is expansive, and it needs no specific object.[1]

Some have described love as the ultimate religious experience. It revels in the perpetual goodness that being in a relationship offers. Love is doing everything with a joyful heart and without trying to escape our pain. In deep love there is awe, mystery, gratitude, sorrow, rapture, ecstasy, grace, luminosity, and sacredness. The flood of emotions runs deeper than deep and more expansive than whole. Love knows no limits. The love-inspired person displays a nobility of character, and his or her virtues flourish! Witness a mother's love for her newborn, lovers in love, a person grieving the death of a beloved friend, a child reveling in the birth of kittens. When people belong, everything seems to fall in place, even in times of chaos and doubt. When intimacy is profound something inside of us says, "This is it."

3

True love defies all words. It is indescribable. When it is there, no words are necessary.

Hints of the idea of deep-partnership love appeared at the beginning of the twelfth century, when courtly or passionate love for another, rather than being considered sinful, was viewed as love emanating from the soul. Passion meant suffering. *Eros*, our longing for physical union, united with *agape*, the universal spiritual love of our neighbor, and became *amour*, a profound personal love relationship. This profound feeling precedes any physical union. With amour, touch and sexuality are sacred.[2] This experience is in complete contrast to the lover of euphoria or the lover of a sexual high. There, pleasure is the only goal. In healthy love, the senses are honored and respected as a meaningful part of the love relationship.

Many writers in the nineteenth century considered the love of a good friend as purer and more noble than the love of the opposite sex. It was not uncommon to use the word *lover* to mean a friend. In an 1841 essay, Ralph Waldo Emerson writes, "High Thanks I owe you, excellent lovers, who carry out the world for me to new and noble depths, and enlarge the meaning of all my thoughts." Emerson asserted, in his essay "Friendship," that "friendship, like the immortality of the soul, is too good to be believed."[3] Friendship to the Transcendentalist writers, such as Walt Whitman, could be an ethereal and physically intimate experience. In his 1888 poem "America," Whitman saw intimate friendship as the nation's hope in the face of the pre-Civil War corruption our government was experiencing. "For You O Democracy / I will make the most splendid race the sun ever shone upon, / I will make divine magnetic lands, / With the love of comrades."[4] Whitman understood that deep affection for others is one of the highest expressions of which we are capable. Yet, even our friendships can harbor elements of addictive love.

Real love can actually be experienced or felt as emanating from the heart. Many spiritual schools emphasize how the heart is the bridge between our human experience and our spiritual experience. As Charlotte Kasl said: "We don't find love by chasing after it; we simply open our hearts and find it within us."[5]

But as we will see, most hearts have been injured, and it is an un-healed heart that can lead to the unhealthy attachments to people, euphoria, romance, or sex that we will refer to as "love addiction." Think of the heart as having two sets of emotions. The lower emotions are connected to the hurts and injuries that lead to placing conditions on the love we offer to others. But our conditions are rarely fulfilled, and the result is that we end up feeling lonely, isolated, anxious, jealous, heartbroken, abandoned, rageful, insecure, hated, hateful, distant, and numb. As we get to the source of these feelings and start learning to integrate them we begin to feel the higher emotions of the heart, those that lead to the deep unconditional love of which we are capable.[6] When that happens we are no longer dependent on our relationships to feel good. We want to reach out, share, embrace, give, nurture—all in the name of love. And a natural greening of Eros occurs.

The first love we experienced came from our parents. Ideally, a parent's love unconditionally affirms a child's worth and life. The mother and father readily and easily fulfill the child's needs and give the child the feeling, "It's good to be alive! It's good to be me! It's good to be with others!" Love feels terrific!

Addiction

Stanton Peele and Archie Brodsky, authors of *Love and Addiction*, define addiction as "an unstable state of being, marked by a compulsion to deny all that you are or have been in favor of some new and ecstatic experience."[7] Any activity that can influence or shift our subjective experience holds addictive potential. Though professionals remain uncertain about the biology of addiction as they continue their research, they seem to be in greater agreement in the area of clinical diagnosis.

Clinicians have found that an addiction compromises three elements: continuation of a behavior despite adverse physical or psychic consequences; obsession or preoccupation; and a feeling of being out of control. Two other elements that may or may not be present are tolerance (progressively needing more of the object of addiction in order to get the same effect) and withdrawal symptoms. What these characteristics suggest is that what constitutes an addiction has more to do with how the object of addiction impacts a person's life than it does with the quantity of that object consumed or experienced. Though there remains controversy among addiction professionals as to whether to accept processes, or behavioral compulsions, as addictions, using current standards emphasizing the above behaviors, we can see how sex, love, and romance qualify as objects of addictive behavior.[8] Several researchers have shown that the euphoria produced by process addictions is the same as that produced by drug or substance addictions. According to Harvey Milkman and Stanley Sunderwirth, "We can become physically dependent on the experience of arousal, satiation or fantasy, independent of whether the capsule for transport is a substance or an activity."[9] Any activity, including love, that evokes any of these three sensations— arousal, satiation, and fantasy—bring about alterations to the brain chemistry.

Our brains provide us naturally with the three sensations of pleasure as a way to experience life more fully. These three planes are controlled by hundreds of brain chemicals that we are only at the beginning stages of understanding. Without these chemicals we would not have the ability to appreciate our own human nature. PEA, for example, is a neurochemical that produces arousal states; it helps keep us alert and motivates us to action. Discomfort states, also produced by the activity of neurochemicals, help us identify our basic human needs so that we seek satisfaction. Chemically controlled feelings of satiation then tell us we have had enough, and allow our bodies to go into homeostasis, or balance. Contentment, creative passion, fear, sexual excitation—each has neurochemical analogues.

Addictions tap into one or more of these same pleasure planes or "feel good" chemicals. Some people crave arousal and exhilaration and get caught up in anything that is dangerous, risky, stimulating: compulsive gambling, illicit affairs, driving at high speeds, mountain climbing. Others opt for a rich fantasy life and soon get lost in it.

Marijuana, psychedelics, mystical preoccupation, objects of romance, and romance novels are all means of tapping into or enhancing our neurochemical "highs." Still others feel "too much" and want a sedative to numb the pain, stress, and fear. Endorphins—the opiates of the mind—are the neurochemicals that kill pain and reduce anxiety. People seeking sedation stimulate endorphins by compulsive food, alcohol, or opiate use, or by pursuing trance-like altered states of consciousness. One very effective way to combine the benefits of more than one neurochemical—a way to avoid pain, live out fantasies, and feel fully alive—is to participate in a love relationship.[10] The problem is, these benefits of our own brain chemistry can be addictive.

For our purposes, we will define addiction as a habit that has gone unconscious; a compulsive ritual that is no longer a choice; a psychological or physical attachment to the object, often characterized by withdrawal, or intensity of symptoms, when the object is removed. Focus on the object of addiction causes an interference with the normal social, occupational, recreational, emotional, spiritual, and physical aspects of a person's life. There is a minimizing, or blatant denial, of the abuse or pain resulting from this focus, and there remains a continued involvement with the object in spite of negative consequences. Love addiction is a malignant outgrowth of our normal human inclination for arousal, fantasy, and satiation.

Our needs are legitimate. Sometimes, however, when getting our needs met takes time and attention away from other important life concerns, our needs become addictions. Words we often associate with addiction include *obsessive, excessive, destructive, compulsive, habitual, attached,* and *dependent.* And when you think about it, some of those words are also used to talk about love relationships. Does this mean love is a habit we have to kick? No, not at all. Our need to experience love is real—our purpose is to identify and then keep unhealthy addictive elements out of our love lives and bring healthy love in. Love relationships are not black and white, either/or, but have all of these elements. Most love relationships seem to have the characteristics of both addictive love and healthy belonging. There are healthy and unhealthy dependencies.

Most of our habits and practices that might have elements of addiction are not unhealthy. Many things we believe we need we really do need for biological survival, and they deserve our attention. We need food, shelter, physical touch and other forms of physical stimulation, recognition, and a sense of belonging. Many of the other things we think we need are merely wants—we can survive without them. Though we need a house, we do not need one with a three-car garage!

When we consider love, the question of need becomes much more complex. Recently, I heard someone say we don't need love in order to survive. And it is true that even a dependent infant doesn't need love to physically survive; what the infant needs is attention and care that activate the body's nervous system and stimulate growth. A baby given adequate physical though unemotional care that includes being touched will survive as well as one given very tender care. But a baby who is seldom touched or not touched at all may get sick, depressed, or in severe cases, become mentally retarded or die.

Thus, in the most primitive sense, we don't need love to biologically survive. But without the experience of being loved as a child, the recipe for a whole, healthy human being is sadly incomplete. Without love, one may live, but may have difficulty developing self-esteem, love for others, or even love for life—all basic ingredients of healthy, nonaddictive love relationships.

Yes, people can live without love, but those I encounter who have difficulty loving themselves or others are usually people who were deprived of nourishing parental care and unconditional love as children. Unconditional love is a love that says to a child, "I love who you are no matter what, even though I may not always like what you say, think, or do." Though there are conditions on behavior that serve as protective fences keeping the child from harm, unconditional acceptance of the child's uniqueness is always present in unconditional love.

Love relationships can be good or bad, depending on how they serve us. The questions we consider here are these: Does love addiction really exist? What is love addiction? How does love become addictive? How can something so wonderful become something that feels so bad? Is it love? Or, is it addiction? What is a healthy relationship?

My clinical experience of love addiction is that it is a reliance on someone external to the self in an attempt to get unmet needs fulfilled, avoid fear or emotional pain, solve problems, and maintain balance. *The paradox is that love addiction is an attempt to gain control of our lives, and in so doing, we go out of control by giving personal power to someone other than ourselves.* This attempt, then, results in an unhealthy dependency on others. It is very often associated with feelings of "never having enough" or "not being enough." This is because many of us did not get all of our needs met in an orderly way when we were children. Addictive love is an attempt to satisfy our developmental hunger for security, sensation, power, belonging, and meaning. Love addiction is also a form of passivity in that we do not directly resolve our own problems but attempt to collude with others so they will take care of us and thus take care of our problems. *We willingly take care of others at our own emotional expense, or we attempt to control them to meet our needs at their expense.* No matter how it plays out, we look to others to "fix" our fear, pain, and discomfort, and we tolerate or inflict abusive behaviors in the process. These others can include any important person in our lives with whom we (often unconsciously) hook up: a child, a parent, a friend, a boss, a spouse, a lover. Or, as in romance or sexual compulsion, it can be someone we don't even know personally. A key element of the unhealthy aspect of the relationship is how we feel when that person disapproves of us, disagrees with us, moves away from us, or threatens us. An escalation in dysfunctional behavior will no doubt occur when the love object leaves or threatens to leave us.

Love addiction may or may not include a romantic or sexual component. When the object of love is, or has been, the romantic and sexual partner, the stakes run high. What we witness daily in the news confirms that the more extreme cases of sex, love, and romance addictions can be lethal. Homicide, suicide, stalking, rape, incest, AIDS, and domestic violence capture the headlines. Love addiction can range from an unhealthy dependency sanctioned by society to violence and abuse abhorred, but never-the-less promulgated by, that same society. It is important to know that these are but degrees of the same problem. We will address the less extreme consequences that touch the lives of most of us almost daily as well as some of the more extreme abuses of love addiction.

Types of Love Addiction

The psychological seeds of dependent love, romance, and sex addiction are sown in early life when we experience overt and covert abuse from those we love. What starts out as healthy dependency becomes unhealthy. The roots of dependent love, romance, and sexual addiction are similar, and often overlap, but the addiction processes of each are unique.

As mentioned above, when a person's object of dependent love is also the object of his or her romantic and sexual desires, he or she will experience intense behaviors when the person/object withdraws or threatens to withdraw. If one considers the millions of people who got high on the daily drama of the O. J. Simpson trial coverage on TV, one can begin to imagine what it is like to be in such a drama itself. The neurochemistry of love can become a drug as difficult to give up as alcohol or cocaine. The number and variety of out-of-control behaviors that result when love is withdrawn are legion. The difficulty with love addiction, however, is that we cannot stop loving or relating! Nor should we! Therefore, we must learn what is love and what is addiction, and when it is that we cross the line from one to the other.

Romantic Love

Romance addiction refers to those times when the object of love addiction is also a romantic object. This object/person can be a romantic partner or live only in the love addict's fantasies. The "fix" may be an elaborate fantasy life not unlike the story line of a romance novel, or the euphoria of a new romance. In either case, the rush of intoxicating feelings experienced during the attraction stage of a romance—a state sometimes referred to as *limerance*—is the drug that can become a substitute for real intimacy.[11] The pursuit of this high can become an addiction in itself. Often, it becomes a dramatic obsession that results in the stalking of the romantic love object by the obsessed person. The love addict seeks total immersion in the romantic relationship, real or imagined. Since the romance-driven high is dependent on the newness of the relationship or the presence of a person, romance addiction is often filled with victim/persecutor melodrama and sadomasochism. Bizarre acting-out behaviors are often a by-product of romance addiction, as the following story demonstrates.

Sharon was a normal seventeen-year-old high school senior. At the store where she worked she met a thirty-year-old man whom she thought a bit strange, but toward whom she acted kindly. Before long, he developed an extravagant romantic fantasy life revolving around Sharon that resulted in letters to her parents proposing marriage to Sharon, stalking her, and a thoroughly imagined future life with her, including a sexual relationship. The more she withdrew, the more out of control his behavior became. As his fantasy life intensified, the letters, threats, and stalking escalated. Sharon and her family lived in terror. Police were called in to deal with the situation. They discovered voluminous notebooks written by the man that read like romance novels. Pornographic drawings and pictures with the name Sharon on them were plastered on his wall. He had become immersed in self-produced doses of pleasurable sensations. In spite of the threat of severe consequences, he was unable to stop his behavior on his own.

Sexual Love

The power of sexual love is unequaled in human experience. In fact, sex may be the only experience that profoundly affects all three of the pleasure planes (arousal, satiation, and fantasy) in our neurochemistry. It has the potential to be the pièce de résistance among life experiences. It is easy to see, then, how sex can become an addict's drug of choice.[12]

According to author and sexual addiction specialist Mark Laaser, a normal sexual love distorted, repressed, or forbidden by religious or familial strictures may result in sexual addiction. He writes that "sexual addiction is a sickness involving any type of uncontrollable sexual activity which results in negative consequences."[13] When obsessive-compulsive sexual behavior is left unattended, it causes distress and despair for the individual and his or her partner and family.

We live in a culture that promotes sex as the drug of choice. All one needs to do is pay close attention to how sexually charged images or situations are presented on television, in magazines, and in film. How often is sex being connected to a deep emotional and spiritual intimacy where body, heart, and soul are relating? Very rarely. There is a staggering amount of denial in our culture regarding out-of-control sexual behavior as pathological; on the contrary, it is glorified. This cultural denial, however, aids the sexual addict in distorting reality, ignoring the problem, and blaming others.

Perhaps the mounting negative social consequences of sexual compulsion will motivate society to take this problem more seriously. People are dying of AIDS; the incidence of sexual violence continues to rise; professionals are publicly shamed and even prosecuted for sexual improprieties and illegalities, and unwanted pregnancies, lost jobs, incarcerations, and broken homes are the results. Sexual exploitation by people in positions of power seems epidemic. The cost of this addiction to our society is more than financial. The fabric of our spiritual, emotional, and relational lives is affected as well.

Patrick Carnes, a pioneer in the field of sex addiction, stresses that sex is not about "good" or "bad," in any moral, social, or psychological context. Rather, it is the behaviors that accompany sex that determine whether or not it is an addiction. According to Carnes, sexual behaviors that involve the exploitation of others—behaviors that are nonmutual, objectify people, are dissatisfying, involve shame, or are based on fear—indicate the presence of sexual addiction.

His research points out some grim facts regarding the possible origins of sex addiction. Of the sex addicts researched, 97 percent suffered emotional abuse as children, 81 percent experienced sexual abuse, and 72 percent reported physical abuse. Such childhood traumas generate core beliefs that become the organizing principles of the sex addict's relationships in adulthood. These core beliefs are: "I am basically a bad or an unworthy person"; "no one would love me as I am"; "my needs are never going to be met if I have to depend on others"; "sex is my most important need"; and "everyone is out for himself or herself." For the sex addict, these trauma wounds must be healed and trust restored before he or she can experience healthy love and sexuality.[14]

Dependent Love

As a psychotherapist, I am acutely aware of how often my clients' adult love relationships exist in the shadow of early love experiences—especially childhood ties to parents.

The story of Anna graphically demonstrates how childhood traumas hover over many adult relationships like powerful, unseen ghosts. While Anna's story may seem extreme, it vividly demonstrates an important truth: there is often more to love than sexual attraction, romance, and relationship compatibility.

Anna, thirty-two, was an attractive, intelligent woman, and the mother of four children. She sought therapy for chronic anxiety and depression. Among the reasons for her melancholy were her troubled, tumultuous feelings for her supervisor, Andrew, who was fifty. Although Anna liked and respected Andrew, she was upset because he had begun to make odd emotional and sexual demands on her. She had come to believe she was in his power and that she could not refuse him—although she did not know why. She only knew she felt a strong obligation to cooperate with him, to try to keep him from becoming depressed. Anna professed love for Andrew, but she did not like his sexual demands, which often occurred at work where his job held power over hers. She knew involvement with him threatened both their marriages, and that the relationship was unhealthy, but she did not understand nor could she control her emotional helplessness when it came to Andrew.

One evening, a distraught Anna called me. She had made a vow a few days before to have no contact with Andrew except on a purely professional basis. But now, he had called her with a plea that she should come to him. In the throes of distress and longing, Anna found her conviction not to see him wavering.

"I feel compelled to see him," she said to me. "My body hurts, I'm shaking uncontrollably, I feel like I'm falling apart—that I've got to see him or I'll get sick or go crazy. Please help me—I feel so helpless!"

I asked her, "Anna, what do you think will happen if you don't see him?"

"I don't know, but it feels like something really terrible will happen, and I'm scared," she said. "And it all seems so absurd!"

I reassured Anna that nothing awful would happen to her. She calmed down a bit, and for the moment, the crisis passed. In a therapy session shortly thereafter, Anna renewed her commitment not to see Andrew. Yet as she said, "I will not see him," her body shook and she wept.

"Why are you so afraid?" I asked.

She struggled to explain. "It seems so crazy. I'm afraid that if I don't see Andrew, if I abandon him, something bad will happen to him. Maybe he'll be so upset that he'll hurt himself. I feel as though he needs me!"

"You're feeling afraid for Andrew," I said. "But Anna, what is your fear for you? You're the one who's upset and fearful. What is it you get out of this relationship? Why are you so attached to this man?"

The answer to that question did not come easily, but in subsequent therapy sessions, as Anna began to relate her childhood, her story offered many clues to her current predicament. The fear Anna felt about Andrew was a familiar one—it was the same fear she once had felt for her father, a man much like Andrew. Anna's father, whom she had seen as a refuge from her mentally ill, violent mother, caused conflicting feelings in Anna. Although he could be a kind, sensitive man, he had made many demands on young Anna—including sexual demands. While Anna's mother neglected her and inflicted violence, her father offered attention and protection—but at a terrible price.

Anna had grown up with an overpowering sense that her father needed her, that he could not do without her, and that she should provide his happiness. Much of her adult depression sprang from her wretched childhood. Anna's pain and guilt as an incest victim also led her to present herself as an asexual adult, but when her sexual feelings were aroused, she could not control the desire and emotions she so vigorously suppressed most of the time. She did not realize that merely because one has sexual feelings, one need not always act on them.

"Why did you believe you had to take care of your father's emotional feelings and sexual needs?" I asked her during one session.

"My dad was the only person I could count on to protect me from my mother," Anna said, relating episodes of emotional and physical abuse inflicted by her mother. She said, "My dad was my protector; he loved me."

Making her father feel good—even though he used her sexually— had given Anna the sense that she was lovable. I urged her to talk about the feelings she had when she acted as her father's servant. In the months that followed, the tragedy of Anna's first experience with love—the experience so mishandled by her father and mother— slowly emerged. It became clear Anna had never separated her love for her father from her agony and guilt over incest. The result was emotional turmoil over her father—and over the concept of love.

During one session, Anna said, "I needed to keep my father around, and to do that I believed I needed to make him happy or he would either reject or leave me. Since I was a child, that meant I would die! What choice did I have but to cooperate with him and try to make him happy?"

There it was—her profound underlying belief that the presence and approval of another person—even one who sexually abused her—meant life itself. And, to some degree, there was an element of truth: Anna the child did need protection! That belief also pervaded her current adult obsession with Andrew; it explained much of her panic and helplessness in the face of his demands.

Consciously, Anna knew she could survive without Andrew. Unconsciously, Anna believed that without Andrew's acceptance, she would not be lovable and her life wouldn't have purpose and meaning.

As a child, she was convinced she needed an intense relationship or she would lose her mental balance—and eventually her life. Our focus in therapy was to prevent an awful history from repeating itself.

In therapy, Anna began to explore her archaic inner self—the dependent, frightened child—that governed so many of her adult emotions, including her penchant for men like Andrew. One by one, she discovered and wrestled with the powerful unconscious beliefs that caused her terror.

"Well, you are no longer four or five, you are grown up. Is that true?" I asked.

"Yes, that's true, but that's not how I always feel. When I'm with this person I often feel like I'm only four or five years old."

"But how old are you?"

"I'm thirty-two."

"And what do you know? Do you actually need this person to protect you?" I challenged.

She thought about it and said, "No."

"Do you need this person to believe you are lovable?"

She hesitated and said, "I'm not sure since I really don't feel very lovable."

"Do you know anyone else who loves you?"

"Yes, I know some other people who love me."

"Does this person give you the only meaning in life?"

She hesitated and said, "No."

"Do you need this person to keep you alive?"

She shook her head, no.

The questions helped clarify her fears and the thoughts that supported those fears. Slowly, she learned the fear and behavior that had made sense to her in childhood no longer needed to have power over her. After some time, she was able to confront Andrew and tell him she would no longer allow him to fondle or harass her. She ended her relationship with him and was able to turn her energies back to her work and family, including coping with marriage problems. Andrew, too, eventually sought treatment for his sexual misuse of female co-workers like Anna.

Anna, whose insecurities ran very deep because of a childhood more troubled than most, must always be aware of her tendency to become obsessed with needy, demanding, abusive men. But she succeeded in handling one such situation and in laying bare the motivations for her behavior. This was no small accomplishment.

Love and the Unconscious Mind

Anna's case may seem rather extreme, but she is not unique. In fact, in family systems such as Anna's, the incest may never be physically consummated, and yet the psychological implications for the child may be nearly as severe in later life. Such cases are sometimes referred to as examples of emotional incest. Over and over again, a child is invited to take care of the parents' feelings. Sometimes the invitation is overt, sometimes it is covert. The child often misconstrues this silent seduction as parental love.[15] When the invitation comes from the parent of the opposite sex, it is covert incest. The parent asks the child to become a surrogate partner. Such partnerships set the child up for a role reversal that later translates into dependent love relationships and confusion about the nature of real intimacy.

Behind each obsessive, often destructive, relationship—which we shall call addictive love—lurks a belief that such dependence serves an important purpose. *To the unconscious mind, addictive love makes perfect sense;* it feels necessary to survival itself. And to an addictive lover, even a pathological relationship may seem normal and necessary. As we understand our fears and the ways we use addictive love, they often lose their holding power.

Addictive love is egocentric and self-serving. Anna, the child, loved her father, not selflessly, but to meet her own needs. She believed she needed her father's attention and approval to sustain her self-esteem—and her life. Although that belief made sense during her childhood, Anna, the adult, no longer needed someone like her father to make her feel lovable and alive. She had her own sustaining qualities, including the potential to love freely, openly, and as an equal. Egocentricity also was evident in Anna's obsession with

Andrew; she believed that without his approval, she would lose the small amount of self-esteem she had and would slide deeper into despair and perhaps even die!

The intensity of love addiction is often in direct proportion to the intensity of one's sense of unmet needs during childhood. Intense love addiction often accompanies low self-esteem. As discussed earlier, such obsession presents us with a huge paradox: we fall into it as an attempt to gain control of our lives, and in so doing we actually grant control to forces outside ourselves. Such willingness to give control away springs from fear: fear of pain; fear of deprivation; fear of disappointing someone; fear of failure; fear of guilt, anger, or rejection; fear of being alone; fear of getting sick or going crazy; and fear of death.

Addictive lovers labor under the illusion that the dependent relationship will "fix" their fears. We will explore the many complex reasons that addictive love exercises a powerful hold over people and why it is not easily given up. Like Anna, many people are drawn into it over and over again. But how do people get drawn into love addiction? The seeds of love addiction lie deep in our biology, our social education, our spiritual quests, and our psychological beliefs. We shall explore each of these in turn.

What you will learn is that each person in an addictive relationship followed an individual road map leading into it. Finding out how love addiction makes sense to its victims is necessary in creating a road map out of love addiction and into mature love and belonging. We return to the puzzle: How does something that feels so good become something that feels so bad?

You will be able to identify all three kinds of love addiction—romantic, sexual, and dependent love—in the stories that follow. Our primary focus, however, will be on the dependent love relationship. It is dependent love to which the human condition seems to direct most of us most often. It is so common that we frequently fail to recognize it until it wreaks havoc on our love lives.

The Roots of Love Addiction

The Role of Biology
The Biology of Bonding

The need to be close to other people—the yearning to be special to someone—is so deeply ingrained in people that it may be called biological. Anthropologist Helen Fisher explains how emotional bonding evolved early in human history to guarantee regular sex and protection of offspring. Such bonding became crucial in the evolutionary process when women lost their period of heat; ovulation was hidden, and therefore, women were more frequently responsive to sex. Women began to bear children more often and needed more emotional support and physical help from men. Males and females began exchanging favors, dividing labor, and tightening the relational "knot." Mating soon went beyond creating offspring. Females began looking for males who were good hunters, who were strong, and who could provide protection that would assure them that their children would grow into adulthood. Males sought the female who was most frequently available for sex in order to guarantee the continuance of his genetic legacy. Eventually, emotional bonding grew beyond mere functional ties to sexual partners and dependent offspring. Both the female and male began rewarding what pleasured and protected them. Babies began bonding with the man who slept with the mother. Personal relationships, the foundation of the family, were established. Along the way, complex rules governing such ties to others developed. With those rules came the fundamental human emotions that lead us to form and preserve our relationships. And it is true that most of the rules and emotions are healthy, delightful aspects of our humanity. To desire, to share, to protect, to nurture, to feel affection, and to live in organic harmony are intrinsic aspects of healthy love. With partnerships and sexual bonding came other emotions as well. Wanting to protect his genetic heritage, the male became jealous and possessive. Fearing that she and her offspring might not survive without the protection of her mate, the female experienced the first fear of abandonment.

Like other primitive fears and habits, many strongly emotional behaviors governing relationships have stayed with us. We still flirt; we still feel infatuation at the beginning of a love relationship, allegiance during it, and sorrow when it fades. We feel guilty if we are promiscuous and jealous or vengeful if we are betrayed. Men still worry about their wives being unfaithful; women still worry about being deserted. We no longer need to bond to guarantee sex or to keep our young alive, yet we continue to do so. Why? To be human, it seems, is to desire attachments to others. Like other behavior patterns from the past—fears of falling, of heights, of closed places, of the dark—the fear of being alone causes panic and despair. The urge to form emotional alliances with others appears to be an innate characteristic—one that makes us human, and one that will no doubt continue.[1]

Our desire for attachment, then, can be viewed as instinctual. As we emerged from the animal kingdom, we developed set responses to our environment. On a biological level, separation can arouse intense anxiety.

The Biology of Attraction

Breaking love down into chemical components may seem to take some of the mystery and magic out of it, but doing so can be helpful in distinguishing between healthy belonging and addictive love. Neurochemical research is showing that anything that generates significant mood change can become an obsession.[2] There are over three hundred chemicals that affect brain function, and we have a working knowledge of sixty. Some of these pertain to our love lives, and it is becoming clear that we can get addicted to the chemical highs that love relationships produce in our brains. The rush of intoxication is now being associated with the neurological release of endorphins or mood elevators. Michael Liebowitz, in *The Chemistry of Love*, states that a specific neurochemical, PEA, is critical to courtship. It produces a high arousal state similar to that caused by amphetamines. Its intense impact seems to taper off with time and when the object of affection is not present. It is interesting to note that PEA has been found to be present in large quantities in people involved in divorce-court trials.[3]

There is considerable evidence that links the high-risk emotions of anticipating danger, fear, excitement, and rage—emotions often present in love relationships—to addiction. Fear can biologically escalate desire.

We carry our own drug supplies within our bodies to help us live a productive life and moderate life's pain. This is nature's way. It is when we become dependent on these inner drug supplies for pleasurable sensations, and our lives go out of balance, that addiction occurs. In love addictions, as in drug addiction, we unconsciously use the objects of love, sex, or romance to thus stimulate the chemicals in our neuropathways to provide the high. Since it is impossible for us to sustain the fix (other people won't always conform their behavior to our neurochemical cravings, after all), we eventually crash and are flooded with feelings of disappointment, depression, anxiety, hopelessness, or powerlessness. To get back on keel, we attempt to use again. Or, when the love object does not sustain the fix, we can develop an obsessive fantasy in which that person is fixing us, or we arouse ourselves with the excitement, fear, rage, or melodrama that exemplify addictive love.

The Biology of Needs

Physically, we strive for inner balance. Infants identify their survival needs through physical sensations and cravings: hunger, thirst, warmth, cold, satisfaction, and irritation. Babies feel discomfort and cry out until there is a soothing response from another person.

When their needs are met, they feel comfort and balance again until the next need presents itself. Life feels good; they feel safe and cared for. They experience trust in themselves, others, and life.

This diagram illustrates an ideal situation.

NEED→	SENSATION→	ACTION→	RESPONSE→	BALANCE
	pain indicates a need (hunger)	reaches out to others (baby cries)	receives satisfaction (baby is fed)	trusts self, others, and life; basis for mature love (feels content)

Sometimes, for any number of reasons, parental care is inadequate—needs are not met and discomfort escalates. Our parents could not always be there as our needs arose. Sometimes we were separated from our parents, and we were cared for by people who seemed strange to us. Infants seem to know instinctively that if certain needs are not met, they will die. In such situations, panic sets in. Now, the situation looks like this:

NEED→	SENSATION→	ACTION→	NO RESPONSE→	NO RELIEF
	pain indicates a need (hunger)	reaches out to others (baby cries)		discomfort escalates; panic felt; sensation suppressed; distrusts self, others, and life. Basis for addictive love.

The recollections of such fearful times are recorded in our nervous systems; we don't ever want to experience such helpless panic again. Adults, too, may be unconsciously convinced that they will suffer or even die if certain compelling needs are not met. Thus arises the intense, often irrational fear and panic when someone rejects or leaves us. Despairing adults seem to forget that they can now take care of themselves, that they can solve most of their problems alone. We have the capacity to think and can therefore postpone needs, problem-solve to get our needs met, or meet our own needs. Often, what we perceive as a need is merely a want and something we can survive without.

Now let's look at a model for adult problem solving.

NEED $\rightarrow$	SENSATION$\rightarrow$	REASONING$\rightarrow$	ACTION$\rightarrow$	RELIEF
OR	OR		TAKEN	OR
WANT	FEELING			GRIEF
		What am I	Do or let go	
		feeling and why?		
		Is it a want or need?		
		Is it realistic and		
		possible?		
		Can it wait?		
		How can I get it?		
		How can I ask for it		
		in ways that consider		
		self and others?		
		What kind of action?		
		What do I do		
		if I don't get it?		

The diagram above—which represents a normal, healthy, adult reaction to a problem—is useful in therapy, where the goal is to help people understand their needs and desires so they may take appropriate action to gain emotional relief or balance. Unfortunately, many of us have learned to deny pain or to limit our problem-solving options; thus, we fail to take reasonable action and we continue to feel physically and emotionally uncomfortable. Instead of reacting logically, we are moved by the infant within us to panic and to cling to another, craving the other to "make us whole" and provide us with a sense of balance. Sometimes, we are not aware of what we need because we have learned to shut off the sensations and feelings of discomfort that identify our needs. Sometimes we feel discomfort, but fail to figure out what we need. Sometimes we feel and reason, but wait in a state of discomfort and fail to take action. And sometimes there is no way to have our desires fulfilled, and we grieve over our losses as a way to regain our balance. At times, our grief is so intense we feel as though we are going to die of a broken heart. The paradox of love is that we must be willing to embrace both joy and sorrow. Many who have loved and felt devastated at love's ending have lived to confirm the words of Kahlil Gibran: "Sorrow carves the heart to contain more joy."

The Role of Culture

For most of his life, Don, an attractive, strong, "macho" man in his late twenties, had denied many feelings. As a boy, he'd learned that he shouldn't cry or demonstrate "sissy" behavior. The only feelings Don expressed often and without inhibition were anger, excitement, and sexual desire. He was ashamed when he expressed tenderness, sadness, or fear.

Don entered therapy because his wife, Peggy, was threatening to leave him. Peggy felt isolated in the marriage; she wanted Don to be more spontaneous and expressive with her. Don was bewildered by Peggy's demands, although he said he was willing to learn how to express tenderness without shame.

Careful examination of Don and Peggy's relationship revealed that Peggy had always been the expressive partner. In truth, she expressed enough emotion for both of them, and at times her emotional behavior bordered on hysteria. Don continued to suppress his feelings because he thought if they both were emotional "something would break." They were caught in a vicious cycle: the less Don expressed, the more emotional Peggy was in an attempt to draw him out; the more emotional she got, the more he withdrew.

Through therapy, the couple learned that because Peggy acted as the feeling partner while Don acted as the thinker—traditional sexual roles—they functioned together as one whole person.

That was troublesome because it limited their individual ranges of expression.

Don had to relearn how to feel and express the whole spectrum of adult emotions; Peggy had to learn enough about herself to feel more calm and confident about her strengths and abilities. Learning to be more expressive wasn't easy for Don; at first he felt "less manly" when he tried to discuss his feelings with his wife. And Peggy found it difficult to learn to think and act for herself. Where did Don get the idea that he had to deny the feeling, nurturing aspect of himself in order to be successful as a man? How did Peggy learn to delegate decision making to Don simply because he was a man? These were questions that had to be examined by reviewing family and cultural role models.

❧   ❧   ❧

As children, we watch how significant grown-ups relate. We learn to respond to certain gestures, smells, idiosyncrasies, styles of dress, and manners. We become accustomed to styles of living, to order or chaos. And we learn the definitions of love, power, and what it means to be a man or woman, definitions that can become locked in our psyches and interpreted in adulthood as universal truths that are not to be questioned. From these definitions, we develop the roles we live out and the base of power from which we operate in those roles. Thus, early acculturation creates a "love map" that is a major factor in determining whom we love and how we love. It doesn't take long before we discover that the map can lead us repeatedly to dead ends.

One thing Western culture teaches us about sex roles is that differences mean inequality or incompleteness and that we need another in order to feel whole. Women were awarded the provinces of sex, beauty, and motherhood (nurturance) as power bases; men were allotted the assertive, thinking realms such as politics, finance, technology, the military, medicine, law, and sports. Real sex differences have been distorted, exaggerated, and misappropriated to create rigid, limiting sex roles for both men and women; we have been acculturated to develop only part of our humanness.[4]

Anthropologist Riane Eisler points out that "not only women, but also men in larger numbers than ever before are taking a close look at their stereotypical gender scripts and rejecting those aspects that limit and distort not only sexual relations but all our relations. . . . Both women and men are beginning to recognize that teaching men to see intimacy as effeminate and to keep score of sexual 'wins'—at the same time that women are taught to believe that their whole lives should revolve around intimate relations with men—is a truly no-win prescription for *both* women and men."[5]

We don't become love addicts in a vacuum! To comprehend how and where we have learned the erroneous ideas about love, romance, and sex that lead to addiction we must examine what our culture teaches us. The messages are both subtle and blatant, and they are ubiquitous and unrelenting. Again, these messages become deeply internalized and unconsciously accepted as fact from an early age.

We live in a culture of image and ownership. We are measured by how good we look, how much we have, and whether we have someone by our side who supports a good image. We have, sadly, been groomed to look outside ourselves for happiness and love. Our obsession with love pervades every aspect of popular culture, from romance novels to rock and pop song lyrics, and even great works of fiction, poetry, drama, and art. You find it on Madison Avenue, in Hollywood, and all the way to Disneyworld. Each day in a variety of ways, our society encourages us to seek addictive relationships. Our culture idealizes, dramatizes, and models a dependency that says we cannot live without another person. Witness the plots of popular gothic romances or soap operas marketed to both men and women; typically, they are odes to consumptive love. When we love, we may naturally feel romantic, but it should be balanced by a healthy appreciation of our independence and self-worth.

Possessive love is a cultural illness in which a person loses himself or herself to an object of love. So powerful is the desire to be with that person that we often behave irrationally. Gradually, we become preoccupied with the love object. Frequently, we feel anxious, crazy, depressed, or lacking self-worth. Eventually, we become distracted from other areas of life—children, work, friends, and spiritual growth. We often mask our self-loathing, self-questioning, and self-forgetting with a quick cover-up scheme. Since we believe that culture dictates our self-esteem, we often project our inner discontent outward in desperate control mechanisms.

Our need to share love is legitimate. That is not the issue. The problem is that our culture has instilled in us such an unrealistic need for others that we sometimes become dependent, addictive, neurotic, or parasitic. We let others dictate our happiness. We become dependent almost unconsciously, and then we resent our dependence. At times we may even become hateful, projecting the hate onto others. Our society trains us to be effective at getting what we want, and when we cannot control others to give us what we want, when we want it, we feel anxious. For proof, all we need to do is turn on the news. In one newscast you can sometimes hear many dramatic stories: "Young woman ends abusive love relationship and is brutally murdered"; "CEO charged with sexual harassment"; "Coach sued for child support by a former lover"; "Domestic abuse charges filed by wife of a professional sports star."[6]

We are all guilty of attempts to control our love lives at times. We must learn how to accept our relationships' limitations and not attempt to control them, for the need to control others is one of the greatest offenses of addictive love.

Love Addiction: Not for Women Only

Men and women have the same need to belong, to be intimate, to experience fulfillment in love. Both have the right to own the feminine and masculine traits that lie within each. Both have a need to experience spiritual and emotional bonding. Both men and women suffer in love relationships.

Loving Me, Loving You

For far too long we have focused on codependency, or addictive love, as a woman's disease. Now, at the dawning of a new century, the result of that misplaced focus is coming back to haunt us. Men adulated as sports heroes are falling victim to AIDS as a result of lifestyles of sexual conquest that, if not explicitly encouraged, are implicitly glorified and admired. Others, distraught with the pain of separation, commit violence against their spouses (or ex-spouses), children, or themselves. It is estimated that one in six men is sexually abused. Some dare not discuss it because it involves another man. If a man is victimized by an older woman, it is dismissed as "scoring." Men's groups have proliferated in order to validate male bonding and to support men in the grief they often feel toward the roles society forces them to play. As we approach the millennium we finally are learning that men actually do have feelings and that women do, in fact, possess souls.

Men are often identified as "love avoidant," but in actuality, love avoidance and love dependence are opposite sides of the same coin and part of the ongoing saga of love addiction.[7] The following story illustrates how the media contributed to one man's confusion.

Rick, a very successful businessman, came into therapy with reluctance. A handsome, congenial man of thirty-six, he believed that he should have the established relationship of his dreams by now. Instead, he was painfully trying to extricate himself from an emotionally abusive relationship. Separation anxiety attacks brought him to therapy. Though he was bright enough to know the relationship was toxic and that he did not know what real love was, he felt compelled to reach out to his former and abusive partner whenever he experienced anxiety. Their sexual relationship was intense, and that pull made it difficult for him to end it. She fit society's description of the "beautiful, sensuous woman," but Rick experienced her as hollow and callous. She lied, manipulated, and sexually betrayed him. The following is an excerpt from his journal.

Although it is starting to change, the conversations I've had with other men [have] been greatly demeaning to women. As Frank Sinatra put it, 'A well-rounded woman is one who has air in her head and a full sweater.' Women as body parts has been a constant theme in my life.

I admit that I have measured the level of love on how pleasing a woman is to me physically. I have mistaken a strong desire by a woman for sex with me as love for me. I think women think of men as sexual objects too; however, they have been conditioned to have totally different issues than men. They have been conditioned to look for security for themselves and for their children. Money is a major factor in women's choices in men (in general). Body parts and physical attraction is a major factor in men's choices of women (in general). When men talk together, they reinforce that tradition. Men comment on whether my new date is "hot" and attractive. They rarely ask what her goals in life are and what she does for a living. They are still much more interested in her looks and sex appeal than her interests. All of this is amply promoted by the media and advertisers. If it isn't sex or image, it's romance.

Everywhere I look—the soap operas, television, magazines, romance novels, advertisements—they all promote dishonest men and glamorous women. Calvin Klein fragrances even has an ad that shows two nearly naked men with one nearly naked woman. Affairs are glamorous, multiple partners are glamorous, lying and cheating is glamorous, divorce is glamorous. With all of this garbage being sold to men and women, how can we ever hope to find a normal, honest, healthy relationship?

I buy many women's magazines to see what is being promoted to women. It's worse than what guys are being sold!

When I see this stuff, it makes me think it's a dog-eat-dog world. I'd better be ready to perform for women, or they'll find a more romantic partner. I'd better learn to hide assets, because even the tamest kitten could be a lioness in disguise. It's a competitive world out there, and romance is a competitive business. That's the overwhelming feeling I'm left with when I see the stuff the media pump out. I've thought of getting a hair transplant because women love thick hair so much. All the male models have thick hair.

Maybe I take all the media stuff too seriously. I do think that it all feeds into our brain and gets stored somewhere. If we ignore it (which takes a lot of energy), it still sits in there and helps form our attitudes in general. At least that's my opinion.

I feel angry at a system that encourages this way of being in a love relationship. And I am confused. Frankly, I do not really know what is love and what is an addiction. At thirty-six and still single I can tell you that I have had some very dramatic and painful love relationships. And I often wonder if I'm a sex addict. Deep inside I yearn for a family and yet I am afraid to risk it. Sometimes I feel like being honest with every woman up front, saying that I'm not interested in marriage, just a passionate, fun, sexual relationship. That way I wouldn't be lying, and the woman who got involved with me would know exactly what to expect. I sound like one of the nineties sitcoms!

Family Role Models

Even our families and peers direct us into addictive relationships. Though those directives are primarily subtle and nonverbal, they are powerful and pervasive. From the time we are very young, we quietly, constantly observe how adults solve problems. We watch, and we seek role models. But often our models lack knowledge about healthy relationships, problem solving, and the importance of individuality and autonomy. In short, Mom and Dad aren't always the best teachers. They have their limitations as well as their talents.

In initial therapy sessions, a client frequently is asked, "If your parents experienced this same problem in their relationship, how might they solve it?" Responses often show that the client has not learned the necessary skills for escaping addictive relationships and nurturing healthy ones based on self-respect. Over and over, people try to solve relationship puzzles without all of the pieces. If you have forty pieces of a one-hundred-piece puzzle, what are your chances of completing the puzzle? Not good! It makes sense to go looking for the other sixty pieces before throwing the puzzle away or proclaiming that you know how to solve it without the additional pieces. Tragically, many would rather chuck the puzzle than seek out the missing pieces. Sometimes, instead, they pretend they have the pieces.

It is no surprise that love relationships are so chaotic at times. Many people grow up in "closed" families—that is, families in which the children are expected to believe and behave as their parents did. Often that's perfectly okay, but when learned reactions to problems lead to unhappiness and frustration, it is time to go outside the family to learn new, more effective ways to resolve conflicts. The mind is like a computer—it collects and stores data and programs to be used when needed. If a computer has inadequate data or no program at all, the problem cannot be resolved.

The Role of Spiritual Quests

Many would say that experiencing our spiritual nature is as profound an experience as we humans can feel. We do not need to have an involvement in a specific religion, though that can play a role. Spiritual pursuits may be defined as those that transport a person beyond material needs and worldly pleasures on a very personal, profound quest for meaning that aligns him or her with a higher purpose for living. Our spirit seeks to continue growing. Like the blade of grass that pushes through hard dirt to reach toward the sun, we, too, continue to quest for the experience of awe, wonder, mystery—union with God. In spirit, we can experience love everywhere and in everything. When we become intimately involved with something or someone, we experience a growing love for that thing or person—the ocean, a sunrise, a painting, our children, a lover, a friend, our creative pursuits, and even an enemy.

Spiritual questing is meant to guide us to stop looking outside of ourselves for happiness. Instead of regarding love relationships as our source of happiness, we can see them as places to express and share our happiness as well as other higher emotions: compassion, sorrow, gratitude, and joy. Love is generated from within. From a spiritual perspective, we are mere conduits of love and we desire to share it. When we participate in shared love, we experience a sense of "oneness" or "unity consciousness." We experience ourselves in the other and the other in ourselves.

In this sense, the soul longs to share itself. Once we know that we are capable of such a "divine experience," we seek it. Some even become addicted to the spiritual high of ecstasy, bliss, awe, and transcendence and choose to live more in that reality than in practical daily life. Though it is natural for us as spiritual beings to yearn for transcendent experiences through which we merge with something greater, this must come through a gradual and balanced process. Some people feel an urgency about these experiences, and their experiments result in highs not unlike those resulting from experimentation with chemicals. When the spiritual "turn on" is the goal, a person can become addicted. Spirituality is not an escape from the world but a way to live in it. When we try to use spiritual searching as yet another form of escape from the painful realities of life on the planet, the result can be devastating. The mass suicide of the Heaven's Gate group provides a sobering example.

Because few people have learned how to develop their spirituality, love addiction may be embraced in the misguided belief that one dependent merging with another is the highest spiritual experience. And it is easy to understand how this might happen, for at the beginning of a love relationship, one often feels euphoria and ecstasy of almost mystical proportions, and rational thought is subordinated.

Self-Actualization

Psychologist Abraham Maslow, who believes that theories of personality and motivation must emphasize healthy, normal development, has proposed a needs hierarchy to describe development from physical, instinctive motives to more rational, transcendent ones. Maslow's theory of "self-actualization," useful in understanding the importance of spiritual questing, states simply that humans tend to move toward being all they can be. Maslow's pyramid of human strivings is illustrated here.

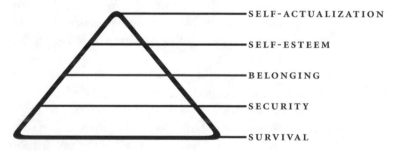

SELF-ACTUALIZATION

SELF-ESTEEM

BELONGING

SECURITY

SURVIVAL

Listed here are the characteristics of people who are near self-actualization.

1. They accept reality.
2. They accept themselves, other people, and the world for what they are.
3. They are spontaneous.
4. They are problem-centered rather than self-centered.
5. They have an air of detachment and a need for privacy.
6. They are autonomous and independent.

7. Their appreciation of people and things is fresh rather than stereotyped.
8. Most have had profound mystical or spiritual experiences, although those experiences are not necessarily religious in character.
9. They identify with humankind.
10. Their intimate relationships with a few specially loved people tend to be profound and deeply emotional rather than superficial.
11. Their values and attitudes are democratic.
12. They do not confuse means with ends.
13. Their sense of humor is philosophical rather than hostile.
14. They resist conformity to the culture.
15. They transcend the environment rather than just cope with it.[8]

Maslow distinguished between two types of self-actualizers: nontranscenders and transcenders. Nontranscenders were "practical, realistic, mundane, capable, and secular." They were healthy reformers of life but had no experience of transcendent "highs." Transcenders, on the other hand, "had illuminations or insights" that motivated them to transform their lives and the lives of others. They felt a sense of destiny, sought truth, did not judge, and viewed pain, even in their love lives, as an opportunity to grow. Maslow considered peak experiences, mystical visions, and self-creation as natural parts of our higher circuitry.[9]

While our human nature focuses on survival and security, our spiritual nature seeks personal growth and fusion with others. Maslow believes that nature recognizes our need to belong, our need to be part of the human group.

Obsessive erotic love often is a misplaced attempt to achieve that fusion we so deeply desire. We want to end the feelings of isolation caused by our learned restraints against true intimacy. In a sexually aroused state, one often is willing to suspend those restraints in order to merge with another. If the merger is dependent and immature, the result is a barrier to self-actualization. Life energy is directed toward the pursuit of gratification rather than toward growth. As Erich Fromm said, "This desire for interpersonal fusion is the most powerful striving in man. It is the most fundamental passion, it is the force which keeps the human race together.... Erotic love ... is the craving for complete fusion. It is by its very nature exclusive and not universal." Without agape, universal love of others, erotic love remains narcissistic. Cary's story depicts this truth.

Adopted as a child into a family that gave him little love or emotional support, Cary had suffered sexual, emotional, and physical abuse. As a result, he vowed he would never get close to anyone, for to do so was too dangerous—or so his childhood experiences had led him to believe.

But as a young adult, Cary struggled with his need to bond with others, a need that had been thwarted by his self-protective promise. The one way Cary felt able to be close to another was through sex. His relationships were shallow, sexually motivated, and short-lived. Again and again, Cary complained of a sense of emptiness and of a longing to be close to someone for whom he cared and who cared for him.

To be sure, erotic love beautifully complements spiritual love in mature people. But sadly, for many, sexual desire often is nothing more than an attempt to relieve the fear of aloneness, to try to fill a void. In that sense, such love is addictive.

The Role of Psychology

Love addiction also can spring from an unconscious search to meet unfulfilled childhood needs and to reinforce powerful childhood beliefs. Each of us acts out a drama that seeks to answer the questions, "Who am I?" "Who are these others?" "How do I get what I need in life?" The drama is not played out in the conscious mind, yet it affects our conscious thoughts, emotions, choices, and behavior. The drama stars myths, roles, and restrictions designed by us in childhood to address early survival needs. A self-promise like Cary's—made in a moment of emotional trauma—may rule our behavior. In childhood, we assessed the world as best we could to determine what to do or not do to ensure comfort and survival. And for some—like Cary—that meant limiting their capacity for intimacy, autonomy, and spontaneity.

All of us believe we know who we are. Yet we are not really conscious of what we are; what one knows about oneself is but the tip of the iceberg. One's life experience is recorded in the body's nervous system. From early experiences, good and bad, we combine our perceptions into logical beliefs on which we make adult decisions. Those include, of course, decisions—conscious or unconscious—about love. In our lifetimes, we will use but a small portion of our physical, emotional, intellectual, and spiritual potentials, all of which play a role in true love. Why do we limit ourselves so? And how does this limitation relate to love? The answers to these questions can be helpful to our understanding the psychological roots of love addiction.

3

The Psychology of Love Addiction

I work with many people who have gone through chemical dependency treatment, diet clinics, or stop-smoking programs—and who have had several unfulfilling love affairs. Many who have exorcised one troublesome behavior pattern find they still harbor compulsive urges to continue an addiction or to substitute something else for it. Intellectually, they may understand such behavior is self-destructive, but physically and emotionally, they still are drawn into it.

When a person gives up one addiction only to substitute another for it, he or she reveals an addictive personality. If such behavior occurs time and time again, one should seek outside help. There is a psychological reason for unhealthy dependency on people. Discovering the psychological basis for such behavior is necessary in overcoming it. As stated earlier, psychological addiction appears to result from unfulfilled dependency needs and an unconscious quest to get those needs met.

Karen's story reveals how several kinds of compulsive behavior may appear in one individual.

❧ ❧ ❧

Karen, thirty, had experienced several dependent relationships in adolescence and young adulthood. Her love affairs usually were emotionally harrowing and often involved physical abuse; Karen tended to fall for men who would use her sexually and abuse her emotionally.

When Karen entered therapy, her self-confidence was low.

Although she had a delightful personality, a keen mind, and a beautiful face, she was 150 pounds overweight. She hoped to learn why she was unable to lose weight and keep it off, for she had been on several diets and at times had succeeded in attaining the body image she wanted—average weight and good body tone—only to have the weight creep back in a few months.

Karen also spoke of her yearning for an enduring love relationship with a man. But at the time, she was strongly attracted to another abusive man, a former lover, now married, who would call her now and then and whose invitations she accepted.

In the course of therapy, Karen was asked to write a letter from her "fat self" to the part of her that wanted a slender, healthy body. She wrote: "If I keep you fat and unattractive, you won't have to experience the fear of beginning a relationship. You won't have to feel uncertain and anxious to please. I can keep you from the pain inflicted by the kind of men you are attracted to—cads! You always become involved with overly macho men who dominate you until you become resentful, or you choose men who are far too needy. I can't trust you to choose a good man, so I protect you by remaining fat. I won't go away until I trust that you won't keep hurting yourself!"

Karen's letter revealed her deeply held belief that her food compulsion—the addictive side of her personality—served as a protective friend. Karen's food addiction was an attempt to shelter herself from abuse and pain, and paradoxically, her obesity exposed her to more of the very thing she was trying to avoid. Feeling shame about her overweight body, she did not believe anyone would find her attractive. She was easy prey to anyone who showed her sexual attention. Karen needed to develop self-worth and personal power. Therapy emphasized the restructuring of her feelings and beliefs about herself, not her weight.

On an unconscious level, addictive tendencies may function as misguided sources of protection, as warped, ineffective aids to emotional stability and survival. The goal of all good therapy and self-help books is to provide tools to help people like Karen live less frustrating, more fulfilling lives, independent of a therapist.

A Psychological Understanding of Dependencies

Transactional analysis, developed in the 1950s and 1960s by Eric Berne, is a model of personality development that has proved especially effective in understanding addictive relationships. It can be helpful in rooting out the underlying life drama that sustains addictive behavior. In the following pages, there is a brief outline of some of the principles of this system that are useful in understanding how our life dramas are related to love addiction.[1]

Transactional analysis divides our personalities into three distinct parts: the Parent, Adult, and Child ego states.

The PARENT EGO STATE structures, nurtures, and protects.
The ADULT EGO STATE thinks and solves problems.
The CHILD EGO STATE feels and identifies needs.

Child Ego State

The Child Ego State is the first part of our personalities to form and the only one we have at birth. It is the source of our strongest sensations and feelings. In our Child Ego State, we experience life primarily through our senses—through strong feelings and desires. It is the Child Ego State that identifies what we need and want and that reaches out to the world, trusting to get the needs met. Long before "inner child" became a buzz phrase, transactional analysts knew of its importance. The Child Ego State is where the myths that support love addiction begin. "It's not safe to get close," "I'm not lovable," "Love hurts," "Men can't be trusted," and "Women are manipulators" are some examples.

Adult Ego State

The second part of the personality to unfold, the Adult Ego State, acts much like a computer, collecting information, processing it, and giving answers. Rational problem solving, not emotion, is its hallmark. If the Adult Ego State receives accurate information, it will provide workable solutions. Unfortunately, the information is often inaccurate; merely operating in one's Adult Ego State is no guarantee that solutions for problems will work.

Parent Ego State

The third and last part of the personality to form is the Parent Ego State, the function of which resembles that of a parent. It is a master plan consisting of guidelines, rules, and permissions for living. It provides protection from harm. It tells us what to do in order to live productive lives. Sometimes it controls, criticizes, and stunts the childlike part of us.

There are three kinds of relationship dependencies we may experience, but not all are addictive. Grown-ups have access to all three ego states, but children do not. Obviously, infants can't think or protect themselves; they form a healthy, necessary dependency on their parents and, with them, function as one person. They borrow their parents' Adult and Parent ego states until they have their own. In a normal, healthy, child-parent relationship, the parent provides love, protection, and nourishment. This is called a *Primary Dependency*. It is necessary if the child is to thrive and develop the ability to be intimate, spontaneous, independent, and, finally, interdependent. *Autonomous Dependency* assumes two adults have all three ego states available to give and receive in healthy ways. But for the child to move from absolute dependency to autonomy, his or her specific needs must be met at every stage of development by the parent figures. At each stage of development a child needs to have important experiences and hear words that affirm the child's worth, abilities, and rights.

Since few, if any, of us get everything we need from our primary dependency in infancy and childhood, a secondary system develops as we strive for survival and growth. This dependency, which I refer to as the *Addictive Dependency*, is the basis for adult addictive relationships. Think back to Anna, whose abuse-dominated childhood made it difficult for her to learn self-esteem and self-sufficiency. Such a system dominated her adult behavior as she took care of others with the belief that in so doing, she would gain esteem and self-sufficiency.

The Child Within: Addictive Dependency

The Child Ego State is worth further scrutiny because it is important in our examination of love addiction. Within that state, Berne says, there are three components: the Natural Child, the Little Professor, and the Parent in the Child.

At birth, only the Natural Child is present—the source of sensations and feelings that tell us what we need to survive. The Natural Child spontaneously reaches out to the world in hopes of getting what it needs. And it will continue to do so unless it is stopped, ignored, or scared.

At about six months, the Little Professor appears. This creative, intuitive aspect of the personality explores the world to answer the question, How do I keep people around? The Little Professor, the master of childish calculation, is driven by the innate urge to survive. The Natural Child knows it needs certain things—food, elimination, warmth, protection, stimulation, touching—to stay alive; in short, the Natural Child knows that *it must keep those big people around in order to survive.* It is the Little Professor's job to answer the question this knowledge raises: *How to keep them around?*

At the age of three, the third part of the Child Ego State—the Parent in the Child—develops. This stage, which lasts until age six or seven, is the kingdom of myths and magic, of Santa Claus, bogeymen, and monsters. Thus, when your mother said, "You make me so mad!" or, "You make me feel so good!" you took her literally; you believed you had the power to control her feelings and she controlled yours. You thought in black and white—no gray—because that was the only way your mind could work then. The Parent in the Child is the holder of myths, which it believes to be truths, that sustain addictive love.

Here's a story from my childhood—but maybe it's from yours, too.

I remember when I was about four I was told that if I crossed the street without permission, something bad would happen to me. I was sitting on the curb with my five-and-a-half-year-old sister one day, and I could see there were no cars in sight. I said, "I bet nothing bad will happen if I cross the street." Despite my sister's protests, I ran across the street and back.

"See? Nothing happened! Yet, my bravado did not run deep; I wasn't sure that something bad wouldn't happen because of my misbehavior—a gnawing fear crept through me.

That afternoon, our family was riding in the car when a siren blared. I panicked and asked, "What's that?" My father quipped, "Oh, it's the police. I suppose one of you kids did something bad." I was terrified; I had been caught! I tried to hide under the seat. My parents had no way of understanding my tears and screams and how my small, magical mind was interpreting events, because they didn't know what had happened earlier.

When they finally were able to question me, they helped me separate my misguided conclusions from reality. They assured me that I was a good girl even if I had misbehaved once; that the sirens were headed for a fire; that sometimes it was dangerous to cross the street. They explained their warning had been given because a neighbor child had been hit by a car.

Calming me with explanations and reassurances, they helped me separate "pretend" thinking from reality. I was not old enough to do this for myself. Had my parents scolded or spanked me, I might have believed I really was bad.

The word *sometimes* is very important to young children, who often think in absolute terms—*always, forever, never*—that lead to adult delusions. Four- and five-year-olds—and some adults whose parents didn't explain things as well as mine did—believe strongly that they must not do certain things, things that often are completely all right, or they will endanger themselves and others.

The Natural Child knows it needs something; the Little Professor figures out how to get that something; and the Parent in the Child carries out the plan of action to keep that something—those essential people—around. In a child, such dynamics are perfectly normal. In an adult, they can be troublesome when they sustain beliefs that turn love—that most precious of human emotions—into unhealthy dependency.

The Myths behind Love Addiction

Behind each addictive love relationship lurks a childhood story dominated by magical thinking and strongly held myths. One such story is Brent's.

❧   ❧   ❧

Brent was a financially successful professional, well respected in the community, who came into therapy with high self-esteem. His problem was his inability to establish relationships that met his needs for support and closeness. He seemed to have a pattern of selecting women whose needs were so great or who were so independent they would not respond to his needs. Intellectually, he was aware of his patterns and selections; still, he was unable to understand them. In exploring his background, much of which he had consciously forgotten or dismissed as not important, the following story emerged.

One ordinary day, four-year-old Brent hugged his mother and ran outside to play and explore; life felt good. Time passed, and as children do, Brent went home for his periodic check-in with Mom to assure himself that his world was in order. When he walked into the house, he found his mother crying, holding his baby brother, who was also crying. (Although Brent had no way of knowing it at the time, his mother and father had just argued over the phone.) Brent's world suddenly seemed threatened, and he felt terror. *What have I done or not done?* he asked himself. Looking for comfort and reassurance, Brent asked, "What's wrong, Mommy? Is everything okay?" Brent's mom said, "Oh, honey, I'm so glad you're here. Tell Mommy everything will be okay." Brent felt momentary confusion and then quickly acted on his mom's suggestion. He patted her arm, smiled into her eyes, and proudly and magically said: "That's okay, Mommy, everything will be all right. I just know it!" Mother smiled and said, "You are my wonderful little man. I don't know what I'd do without you."

❧   ❧   ❧

Brent's world was in order once again. But something significant had happened. The four-year-old boy could not perceive that the incident was a natural and isolated occurrence and that the comfort he offered his mother was not the result of some magical power he possessed. A myth was born and grandiosity established: Brent began to believe that somehow he had the power to make his mother (and perhaps everyone) feel good; moreover, he had to do so in order for his own needs to be met. The child-belief that prevailed was: "I'm in charge of making people feel good or bad; what I say, think, feel, or do will keep them around or drive them away."

Brent's childhood story may sound rather poignant and sweet: a child caring for his melancholy mother. But Brent was a child who needed his mother to be a big person who would care for him. Like other children of this age who are as yet unable to separate pretend from reality, he feared that if something happened to his parents, his world would not last. He also believed he might be the cause of his mother's pain; parents often unwittingly say things like "You make me feel bad" that a child takes quite literally. As an adult, Brent would have responded to the situation by reasoning, *Mom is upset. I'll offer her sympathy, though I can't make everything better.*

As a child, Brent needed information and reassurance he didn't receive. He needed Mom to say: "Thank you for caring about me and I'm fine." Instead of receiving maternal comfort for his *frightened* Child Ego State, Brent was invited to take care of his mother's *sad* Child Ego State, *suppressing his own fears and needs in the process.* Brent had cared for his mother at his own emotional expense; he continued to do so in his adult relationships. From a child's point of view, Brent's decision was creatively adaptive: *I'll stop feeling scared and needy and take care of her.* And it did seem to work! Mom did stick around. And she even smiled!

Because Brent continued his unconscious pattern of suppressing his feelings and needs, he would unconsciously choose needy women who supported his belief system. Thus, he actually had what he wanted in his troublesome addictive relationships; they were psychologically self-serving. Dependent partners prevented him from having his own needs fulfilled. In a variety of subtle ways, his partners supported his earlier conclusions: *My needs are not important,* and *I have the power to make a woman (Mom) feel good.*

The tragedy is that Brent needed and had a right to his own feelings, desires, and support; he needed to be cared for without always having to care for others first.

In love addiction, the ties of dependency run from one partner's inner child to the other's inner child. Something within addictive lovers makes them believe they need to be attached to someone in order to survive, and that the other has the magical ability to make them whole. This is why love often goes wrong. Addictive lovers don't believe they can be whole alone. The pervasive feeling that something is missing directs them in adult relationships to unconsciously seek out others to meet their unmet needs. The difficulty is that a person out of touch with what his or her real needs are tends to seek out people similar to the original person (i.e., a parent) who did not have the capacity or information to meet those needs in the first place.[2] Thus, it is like hitting one's head against a brick wall— a self-defeating exercise.

Only when Brent, like Anna and so many others, was able to examine his unconscious fears and beliefs connected to his unmet needs from a new adult perspective was he psychologically free to establish healthy interdependency with women.

Immature, childish love believes: "If I take care of you and love you the way I want you to love me, then you'll love me that way, too." We may think of a child's love as generous and innocent; but often it is not. Children are not yet capable of spiritual love; their love is egocentric. They love in order to survive, in order to avoid pain, fear, and want. And that pattern, as we're seeing, haunts adult addictive lovers.

Brent's story illustrates the point we made earlier: love addiction is not for women only! There is no one-way dependency; it is always mutual. On a social level, men are thought to be independent or antidependent, and women are thought to be dependent. However, psychologically, men are encouraged to be emotionally empty and therefore dependent; in that realm, it is women who are acculturated to be independent. We often hear that more men than women die, suffer depression, attempt suicide, or find a new partner within the first year and a half after the loss of a partner. As one man told me angrily, "I didn't even know what feelings were before she left me. Now that I have them, I don't know what in the hell to do with them. And where do I go for help? Men don't have close friends, support groups, and God forbid, feelings! It's a damn trick. No wonder men don't get close."

Women have cultural permission to feel, to need, to cry, and even to be depressed and scared. They live longer, develop support networks, and often thrive after their recovery from grief. After all, they are the traditional caretakers. All they need to do is include themselves in their caretaking.

Men also suffer in relationships, but do not always have the support to openly acknowledge the pain and seek help. Men have the same need to belong, to bond, to be intimate, to experience fulfillment in love.

II

How Do I Love Thee?

4

Addictive Lovers

This beast that rends me in the sight of all,
This love, this longing, this oblivious thing,
That has me under as the last leaves fall,
Will glut, will sicken, will be gone by spring.
The wound will heal, the fever will abate,
The knotted hurt will slacken in the breast;
I shall forget before the flickers mate
Your look that is today my cast and west.
Unscathed, however, from a claw so deep
Though I should love again I shall not go:
Along my body, waking while I sleep,
Sharp to the kiss, cold to the hand as snow,
The scar of this encounter like a sword
Will lie between me and my troubled lord.

EDNA ST. VINCENT MILLAY, Fatal Interview

Identifying Addictive Love

Most, if not all, love relationships harbor some elements of addiction. Let's face it—blissfully harmonious, mature interdependency is just an ideal we are striving for. If we are to achieve mature love, we need to have experienced as children the steady, strong parental love that helps us to love ourselves. Parental love gives us a strong sense of well-being and allows us to experience giving for the sheer joy of it. This allows us, as adults, to experience and express our full spectrum of emotions and desires. We can think clearly and separate illusion from reality, and confidently give voice to our thoughts and determine how best to meet our needs. If we are to be capable of mature love as adults, we need to develop an internal system of self-parenting that offers unconditional self-love, wise self-guidance, and strong self-support.

In addition to strong parental love, we need to have grown up in a culture that worked to free its children from the illusion that others hold the key to a life full of constantly fulfilled promises: absolute safety, unearned trust, instant gratification, power, and perpetual comfort. That culture would be honest and admit to us that human beings don't inherently possess all of the tools needed to form conscious, intimate relationships with others—that we are in need of constructing a whole new curriculum. Contrary to what the Beatles song would lead us to believe, this curriculum would say love is not all you need, and living love is not easy. Love asks much of us. The curriculum would say "go easy on yourself; a conscious, intimate, loving relationship has never been done before." It would say that we must watch out for denial and see how our conditioning plays out in destructive ways in our love relationships.

If we all met these requirements for mature love, we'd all be self-contained, yet capable of the kind of love that would satisfy our deep-seated yearning to be close to others. Steady, strong parental love and realistic cultural guidance would nurture mature self-love in children, who would enjoy a sense of well-being and, therefore, be able to experience giving for the sheer joy of it. That's the ideal. Few people are lucky enough to have all it takes to be a completely mature individual and lover. But there is much that adults can learn about love and freedom, and that is our goal here.

Infantile love operates on the principle, "I love because I am loved." Mature love embraces the idea, "I am loved because I am love." Immature love says, "I love you because I need you." Mature love allows for individuality and for free expression of ideas and feelings; it consents to discussion of values—and even, at times, to confrontation. Immature love can be lethal; mature love nourishes.[1]

Elements of unhealthy dependency creep into even the best of mature love relationships. The challenge we face is to identify and acknowledge addictive elements, uncover the myths that support them, do what we can to change them, and build on the best aspects of a relationship. How do we know if our love is an addiction? For the answer, let's take a look at twenty prominent characteristics of addictive love.

The Characteristics of Addictive Love

People in addictive relationships have the following characteristics. Some have a few. Some have many. Generally, they

1. often feel consumed
2. have difficulty defining ego boundaries
3. exhibit sadomasochism
4. have difficulty letting go
5. fear risk, change, and the unknown
6. experience little individual growth
7. have difficulty experiencing true intimacy
8. play psychological games
9. give to get something back
10. attempt to change others
11. need others to feel complete
12. seek solutions outside the self
13. demand and expect unconditional love
14. refuse or abuse commitment
15. look to others for affirmation and worth
16. fear abandonment when routinely separated
17. re-create familiar, negative feelings
18. desire, yet fear, closeness
19. attempt to "fix" others' feelings
20. play power games

Now, let's look at each of these characteristics in more detail.

Feeling Consumed

We may crave our beloved so intensely that we think, *I must have him (or her) or I can't go on!* This is especially true early in a relationship.

Remember Anna, who experienced actual physical sensations—the shaking—that led her to believe she or Andrew were in danger when she severed her ties to him? Even when the object of our attention is not sexual or romantic, our love consumes much of our mental energy because we are busy deciphering the other's needs and thoughts, planning around the other, and holding back on our own needs and wants. Energy for more important life pursuits is sapped. Our growth is delayed or stifled.

Difficulty Defining Ego Boundaries

This means other people so totally dominate our egos that it becomes difficult to know who is thinking what, which feelings belong to whom, and who is responsible for which actions. Our ego boundaries should be open enough to allow for the free flow of thoughts and emotions, but not so much that our energy is sapped and our identities become blurred with the identities of others.

For example, I noticed with one couple that whenever I asked the husband what he *felt,* his wife quickly answered for him; when I asked her what she *thought,* her husband quickly answered for her. At first, they were unaware they were responding for each other, but they soon realized she was responsible for the feelings in the relationship, and he for the thoughts. Given such an arrangement, it became clear why these two feared separation, for they functioned together as a whole and unconsciously allowed themselves to act as mere halves.

The romantic notion that urges two "to become one" sounds ideal—but this is impossible in real life, and the concept is neither romantic nor an ideal worth pursuing. We don't have to lose ourselves to be close to another person.

Boundary, by definition, refers to a landmark that distinguishes one piece of territory from another. In relationships, it suggests the importance of developing our uniqueness to clearly mark our psychological territory. A fence is an easy dividing line to recognize; psychological dividing lines are more complex. We use words to describe these ephemeral boundaries. "I feel invaded." "I don't know where I stop or another begins."

A healthy boundary is permeable so that it allows a free exchange of thoughts, actions, words, and feelings while serving to protect us from psychological invasiveness. Boundaries can be too weak or too rigid.[2]

Examples of weak boundaries:

- intimate conversations with people with whom you have not established trust
- falling in love with anyone who reaches out
- being sexual solely to meet someone else's needs or desires
- acting on a first sexual impulse
- disregarding personal values to please someone
- accepting things you do not want—food, sex, touch
- failing to recognize when your boundaries have been violated
- failing to stop others from violating your boundaries
- saying "yes" when you mean "no"
- letting abusive people remain in your life
- trusting anyone
- telling all
- adulating others

Examples of rigid boundaries:

- trusting no one
- black-and-white thinking
- compartmentalizing life—keeping people and activities in one's life isolated; failing to integrate various aspects of life
- holding out—refusing to yield or compromise
- putting up a wall—not sharing thoughts, feelings, energy with others; becoming physically rigid, withdrawing
- lacking in empathy
- being intimate only when sexual
- unwillingness to be vulnerable
- feigning emotions
- avoiding love—not accepting caring from others
- living a secret life
- observing life verses fully living it
- exhibiting a hardened attitude—being set in one's ways, constrained, lacking ability to empathize or show feelings

Exhibiting Sadomasochism

In many unhealthy, dependent relationships, one partner generally gives more while the other takes more. Sadomasochism can be subtle, as when one person is the brunt of jokes or is constantly presented as "the problem" in the relationship. One partner may unconsciously enjoy hurting or disappointing the other, while the other unwittingly enjoys being hurt or disappointed. In severe cases, one partner physically abuses the other. Jerry's story is an illustration.

❧   ❧   ❧

Jerry was young, handsome, and virile; he longed for love and contentment, yet he repeatedly chose women who teased and taunted him and betrayed him sexually. As a child, Jerry often had been told he was bad and unworthy of love, and unconsciously he still believed this was true. He chose partners accordingly and endured the emotional pain until, as he put it, he "couldn't stand it." At that point, he would often physically abuse his partner. The resulting damage and guilt only confirmed his feeling of unworthiness.

Jerry's goal in therapy became transformation of his underlying belief that he was unworthy of love. He needed to learn to believe that he deserved love and care so he subsequently would choose truly loving, caring partners.

Difficulty Letting Go

Because addictive love is so intense, there is a fear of letting go. As a result, some clearly pathological relationships may endure for years.

❧   ❧   ❧

Denise and Larry's relationship had been emotionally dead for years. Although they often talked about divorce, they avoided taking steps toward it.

Exploring their dread of divorce in the face of the irredeemable loss of their love, they found that their fear of being alone and lack of confidence in their abilities to cope with separation and change were keeping them together and unhappy. As children, both had been abandoned physically or emotionally by their parents, and neither wanted to relive the pain of loss or rejection. What they had seemed preferable to what they feared.

Denise and Larry failed to trust their individual abilities to be independent, to cope with separation, and to experience fulfilling relationships in the future. They now are separated—a melancholy decision that was nevertheless right for them.

❧   ❧   ❧

We all have experienced loss in our lives, and it hurts. We have been rejected, and it hurts. Most people empower their pain by believing they cannot stand it and by doing everything to avoid it. Rather than facing the pain and trusting it will end, they hang onto unhealthy relationships to avoid grief.

But loss and rejection are part of life; to think we can avoid them is magical, mythical thinking. Grief is a natural, healing response to loss. Contrary to what we might believe, we do have the ability to handle pain. Addictions are a misguided attempt to increase our comfort level.

Fearing Risk, Change, and the Unknown

Another element of love addiction is its apparent safety and predictability. I once asked my young son, "Why do you think winners might have more losses than losers?" He thought about it a bit and said, "Because they take more chances and try more things." And that's true. Winners don't stop when they make a mistake; they don't kick themselves when they lose. They ask, "What can I learn from this? How can I do it differently next time?" But addictive lovers hang on and on and on, because dependent love is safe and predictable—or so it seems to them.

❧   ❧   ❧

Candi sought therapy, she said, "to learn to grow up." She was dating Mike, who accused her of being a baby and a hanger-on. Mike had told her that if she didn't "grow up," he would leave her for another woman he had been seeing. Candi's motive for trying to change was to please Mike; she didn't want to lose him. But Mike did not really want Candi to change. He hoped to justify his relationship with the other woman by blaming it on Candi's inability to grow up. When Candi realized Mike really favored her dependency, she dropped out of therapy, still fearing she would lose him.

A year later she was back in therapy, saying this time it was for herself. She knew she deserved to feel grown-up and happy; if Mike wanted to join her, fine. If not, she felt ready to risk the unknown and move ahead with her life.

Experiencing Little Individual Growth

In addictive love, the lovers stagnate; they often are satisfied with a monotonous lifestyle. They put more energy into concern about their relationship than into personal growth—self-actualization. As Abraham Maslow discovered, humans have a natural urge to grow. When that urge is neglected because of an addictive relationship, we are, in a sense, dying—if not physically, then spiritually.

People wrapped up in dependent relationships are not living up to their potential when they suppress individual gifts and abilities. To deny oneself growth is personal abuse. Such denial often results in emotional or physical illness after stress builds up to a certain level. The reason for this is that we each have a certain amount of energy to be expressed in feelings, thoughts, and actions. Energy has to go somewhere. When it is suppressed or blocked, one of two things eventually happens. The energy will either be directed inward, in which case we will get sick physically or mentally, or it will explode outward and we will strike out at others.

❧   ❧   ❧

Barbara was bright and creative. Encouraged by her husband, Gary, she returned to college after their children came of school age. In time, Barbara obtained a graduate degree and began to expand her interests and activities. In many ways, it seemed she was surpassing her husband's education and success.

Then Gary's insecurities surfaced. He complained that Barbara's job was more important to her than their marriage. Barbara, anxious to please him, began to limit her friendships and activities, and in time, she became ill.

At that point, Barbara and Gary went to see a counselor. Their therapy focused on teaching Gary to explore his fears and insecurities, freeing him to appreciate and encourage Barbara's creativity and success. It also helped Barbara explore her tendency to deny her needs, and to find a balance between the demands of her career and her marriage.

Difficulty Experiencing True Intimacy

What is intimacy? The word *intimacy* has different connotations to different people. For some, it suggests a profound emotional closeness, a deeply personal connection. For others, it is interchangeable with the word *love*. For some, it's a euphemism for "sexual closeness," often suggesting illicit overtones.

If we accept Eric Berne's definition of *intimacy* as a "profound exchange of thoughts, feelings and actions in the here and now," we expand our understanding of intimacy to potentially include all life experiences.[3] Because intimacy, by Berne's definition, is happening now, it suggests an openness, vulnerability, risk taking, and unpredictability we might not like. It does not hide in the past or future. It can feel good or bad. Soldiers in combat feel heightened intimacy. Watching a loved one die is intimacy. Expressing anger to stop hurtful behavior is intimacy. Resolving conflict is intimacy. Domestic abuse is intimacy. It is happening now!

In moments of intimacy, because of one's vulnerability, one absorbs the experience into his or her psyche. Indeed, early childhood trauma was intimacy! In some cases, the pain of intimacy was so great that we may have promised ourselves never to be that intimate again. Such self-promises close us off to more ecstatic states of intimate love.

In intimacy, then, we are naked and free to reveal the truth of who we are, including our emotional wounds, our fears, our walls. In intimacy, relationships are processes, not perfect products. Intimacy— the exchange of thoughts, feelings, and actions in an atmosphere of openness and trust—is a profound expression of our identities that leaves us in a euphoric state. Even under healthy conditions, however, the experience of intimacy is a rare and precious gift. Berne claims we are fortunate if we experience only three hours of sustained true intimacy in our lives. In addictive love real intimacy is almost nonexistent. That is because in true intimacy we are vulnerable and open to hurt and disappointment, as well as ecstasy.

Recall the Natural Child component of the Child Ego State: true intimacy involves contact between the Natural Child in two people. But dependent lovers often suppress that state in their attempts to care for others. And, often, they mistake unhealthy dependency for intimacy. Addictive love gives the illusion of intimacy without our having to be fully vulnerable. That illusion—that we can have human closeness without risk—is a large part of the attractiveness of dependent love. But as with all addictions, the promise is a false one that will always betray us sooner or later.

Playing Psychological Games

What often appears to be intimacy is not. Melodramatic psychological games replace intimacy in addictive relationships. Such games provide interaction and drama and are a roundabout way of seeking fulfillment of our desires and needs. Perhaps you've seen such "acting" between two partners.

Although asking for something in an indirect fashion—through game playing—is less risky than being open and direct, we're also less likely to get what we want this way. Addictive lovers, therefore, often are disappointed. One of three roles is usually adopted by a game player: victim, rescuer, or persecutor. Such games look absurd to outsiders, who often recognize them for what they are, but the games seem perfectly normal to the players. Watch any soap opera on any given day and you will know exactly what I mean. "Does Tom [rescuer] really love Cindy [victim]? Tune in tomorrow." Tomorrow, Tom confirms his love for Cindy, who now has to admit that she is not who Tom thinks she is. She has had to hide her real identity for reasons we do not yet know. By next week, however, we find that she is really Joan, in love with Tom's best friend, Phil. (Now she is the perceived persecutor.) Tom (now a victim) feels enraged and determines to get even with them both (persecutor).[4]

In our more ordinary, less melodramatic lives, the games we play are more subtle and thus not always easily recognized. We may not be consciously aware of game-playing dynamics at all—that is, until we feel the pain they cause. Even then we do not always fully comprehend what happened. Instead, we feel confused. We rally, suppress the pain, and continue the game.

꧁ ꧁ ꧁

Gina and Randy were inveterate game players. Gina was a depressed, sexually unresponsive young woman whose favorite game was "Ain't He Awful?" She was referring, of course, to her husband, Randy, who was very aggressive sexually with Gina—and with other women. Randy's favorite game was "Poor Me," and his self-pitying litany was, "How can you expect me to be faithful with a wife who won't let me touch her?" Gina cited her depression and anger to justify her inability to respond; Randy cited his frustration and anger to justify his unfaithfulness.

In reality, both were actually content with the story line they had concocted. Both were fearful of risky commitment and intimacy, and their games allowed for warped contact, interaction, and melodrama. Meanwhile, they didn't have to cope with their problems or make tough decisions about change.

Giving to Get Something Back

In addictive love, what appears to be altruistic love often is not. Addictive love is conditional; the underlying hope is, "If I do the right things, I'll get what I want." Giving spontaneously often is experienced as giving up, giving in, or losing part of oneself. This occurs because, on an unconscious level, the giver has promised not to grant control to another.

Oftentimes, wrung by sorrow from rejection or loss, we make promises designed to protect ourselves, and our unconscious takes it literally. When you are hurt in love, it's important to listen to what you tell yourself. If you hear yourself saying, "I'll never do that again," say instead, "I'm bigger than this pain, and I will heal and love again." Keep in mind that when you are feeling deeply, you are defenseless, and emotional messages received often become truths that you make to yourself and act on later.

Attempting to Change Others

Because we may experience ourselves as incomplete and therefore seek other people in search of wholeness, love addiction involves attempts to change others and scrutiny of others for faults.

My clients say, "If only Barbara would stay home, I'd be happy"; "If only Gina wasn't unresponsive, I wouldn't act out sexually"; "If only Candi would grow up, I'd be content"; "If only Don would be sensitive, I'd be happy"; "If only women would really love me, I'd be fulfilled at last." Over and over again, people try to change others in an effort to camouflage their own fears and inadequacies.

Candi's partner, Mike, expressed self-confidence, yet his need for dependent, insecure women in his life revealed his uncertainty. After he admitted his uncertainty, he and Candi were able to love each other with more calm and honesty.

Remember, your love addiction fits you like a glove. Stop putting the problem on the other. Why do you need an unresponsive woman? Why do you need an angry man? Why do you work for a tyrannical boss? How does your relationship fit you?

Needing Others to Feel Complete

Addictive love is always mutually symbiotic: the addictive lover needs another to feel whole, balanced, and secure. Anxiety occurs whenever this unhealthy symbiosis is threatened. Often that anxiety explodes into emotional or physical violence, as Hank and Ann's story reveals.

❧ ❧ ❧

Hank was a cold, prejudiced perfectionist. He was groomed to be that way; he grew up in a family that placed great emphasis on looking good on the surface, while in the privacy of their home practiced emotional and physical abuse. Hank's wife, Ann, was warm, insecure, shy, and passionate. Hank bluntly expressed his lack of emotion for Ann: "She is there, but I don't feel anything for her." Whenever Ann questioned the relationship or discussed leaving Hank, he became furious and abused Ann verbally, sexually, and physically. Although Hank clearly did not love or want Ann, he pathologically needed her. The thought of her leaving caused him intense anxiety. Primal feelings of ownership, a well of unmet needs from childhood, and role models that nonverbally said "men get what they want by bullying and staying distant," "men have to control," "women keep men happy," surfaced each time Ann said she had had enough. But Ann had no intention of leaving. In fact, Hank's behaviors were, in a skewed way, welcomed by Ann. They suggested to her that she might really be needed and therefore lovable. She developed an odd sense of security in Hank's perverse behaviors. This is often the paradox of violent marriage: two people feel strongly that they need each other, but slowly destroy each other in spite of—or, rather, because of—that perceived need.

Seeking Solutions Outside the Self

Whether we care to admit it or not, many of us still think magically, like children who believe in Santa Claus, waiting and wishing. Ask yourself how many times you have thought or said the following statements:

"If only I had someone . . ."
"If only he (or she) would change, then . . ."
"When he (or she) has more time, then . . ."
"After the kids are grown, then . . ."
"If I love just a little bit more, then . . ."
"Next year, things will be better."

"After he (or she) is gone, then I'll be happy."
"Until he (or she) shapes up . . ."
"Something is bound to happen soon."
"He (or she) can't stay this way forever."
"I'm waiting for him (or her) to hit bottom."
"I'm waiting for him (or her) to see the light."
"This isn't the real him (or her)."
"I don't have a problem; he (or she) does."
"I wish he (or she) would hurry up and change."
"I hope he (or she) sees me for what I really am."
"If only I had done more, he (or she) wouldn't have left."

Instead of direct, assertive requests or realistic appraisal and action, we cling to our childish beliefs in magic. We must face the fact that there is no magic; we are responsible for ourselves and for our actions. Failure to rely on oneself leads to frustration and unhappiness.

Meghan, a client who tells her story extraordinarily well, is living evidence that waiting and wishing for, and empowering others to provide us our happiness does not work!

Her story shows how addictions—several of them in Meghan's case—can plague people. Meghan endured a series of trials and addictions before she finally quit looking for comfort and relief from outside herself and chose instead to look inward.

❧   ❧   ❧

"Five years ago, when I was thirty-five, I finally went into treatment for longtime alcoholism and began the process of recovery. Sobriety is a miracle in my life. Before I became sober, I tried to avoid all my problems through excessive use of alcohol and other drugs. I coped with life by drinking and eventually became addicted to alcohol. Change could not occur in my life unless the alcohol was removed.

"I grew up in an alcoholic home, and dealt with my unhappiness by being secretive and passive. I acted as a people pleaser in my family. One of the roles I took on was mediator between my mother and father in regard to his drinking. During this time, I was sexually molested by my father. My mother, who knew what was happening, took no action to stop it and chose to blame me, a ten-year-old child. During the fearful years that followed, I clung to the belief that when I finally left home my life would change. I dreamed of escape, and I thought escape would be marriage. I wanted to be rescued by someone stronger and healthier than myself.

"But 'rescue' was not forthcoming. As a young adult, I coped with my pain by being an 'achiever,' and by excelling in music, playing in local music groups. Before performing, I took tranquilizers for my anxiety. I also began to drink heavily. As the result of my very low self-esteem, my music suffered. Most of my social life and contacts involved drinking. I met my husband in this atmosphere.

"When I drank, I felt powerful, in control. I felt high and happy. *So this is how people manage,* I thought. I considered those who didn't drink foolish and unaware of what life was really all about.

"But after a while, I was startled to find alcohol no longer helped me get rid of depression. I found myself slipping into long periods of maudlin weeping. I felt helpless and alone. Mark, my future husband, 'rescued' me. He provided me with alcohol, assumed management of my finances, made decisions for me, and—wonder of wonders—even after I told him about my wretched childhood and history of promiscuous sexual relationships—he still wanted to marry me.

"As our wedding day approached, he began to throw my past at me, resulting in terrible quarrels in which I always ended up crying and begging for his forgiveness. I allowed Mark to use my past as a sort of stick held over my head. I was very sure no one else would have me, and I wanted desperately to belong to someone; I still believed marriage would mean the end of my troubles. I had forgotten my childhood beliefs: "men are abusive and scary"; "no one can ever love me." However, it wasn't long before these beliefs became a living nightmare.

"Only a month after we were married, Mark began to beat me. I once left him for several days, then returned because I believed no one else could love me. I cringe now when I think of how little love I had for myself. I took extreme care to try to please Mark, believing if only I behaved properly, all would be well. The only good result of this self-effacing behavior was that my drinking was curtailed during these years because Mark strongly objected to the amount I drank, and I wanted to please him.

"One way I could feel good about myself was by being a hard worker. After my children were born, I continued to work, partly because my job helped me feel good about myself and partly because I did not trust Mark to provide for us. I passively handed over my paychecks to him; if I needed anything, I had to beg him for it. It never occurred to me that my income was my own, and I could trust myself to handle finances.

"Meanwhile, I continued my role of rescuer, protecting my mother from my father's alcoholic rages. I felt important when I got her away from the house or argued with my father on her behalf. I had no real friends; my time was spent with Mark or my mother. I used my mother to provide me with tranquilizers and antidepressants; Mark would not pay for them, but she would. Mark also would not pay for clothing for me or the children; he said there were bills to be paid. My mother paid for these things too. Nevertheless, I still felt Mark was taking care of me, and although there was no affection between us, I stayed with him out of fear. My mother and I would commiserate together about our marriages.

"I began to realize that my marriage and my way of life were unhealthy, and I asked Mark to see a marriage counselor with me. He refused, and I left him. A few days later, when Mark agreed to enter counseling, we reconciled. We spent the next six months in a counseling group. After counseling sessions, we would go out and drink together, which we had not done since our courtship. Mark no longer objected to my drinking; in fact, he encouraged it. Suddenly, we were both using alcohol to numb our unhappiness. As a result, the counseling was unsuccessful; we refused to face our problems.

"Then my mother died. This was a turning point in my use of alcohol. Even though I knew it was wrong to drink to avoid pain and grief, I drank in defiance of that knowledge. Anything was better than my pain. Now I was drinking large amounts on a daily basis. I was pregnant with my fourth child, and I consider it a miracle that my daughter Daniella was not born with fetal alcohol syndrome. The day before she was born, I was so drunk I could hardly walk.

"One night shortly after Daniella was born, Mark and I got drunk, then got into a vicious argument. He beat me up, saying that during the months of marriage counseling he had been waiting for an opportunity to show me who was in charge. For some reason, I had never seen the brutality of his behaviors before; I was shocked. I knew I could not trust him and I began to fear for my life.

"I decided I had to leave the marriage, but I didn't know how to handle it. I trusted no one; I fell into silence, barely speaking to Mark for months. I continued to drink heavily; Mark was drinking heavily too. Then he got into deep financial trouble because of gambling debts, and he swore off alcohol. In a terrible incident witnessed by our children, he beat me up again. The next day, I took the children and fled. I got an attorney and eventually a divorce. Now, I thought, all my problems would finally end.

"But they didn't. I kept drinking; I chose to be with men just as abusive as Mark. This went on for about three years before I realized I *had* to quit drinking. I tried many times to quit on my own—it never worked. My employer began to confront me about my tardiness and absences, and my work suffered. My drinking was out of control; I avoided people and neglected my children. I often was ill, and it was only through the intervention of a cousin that I finally sought professional help for my drinking.

"While in treatment, I learned a lot about myself. I learned how I had blamed others for how I was. I learned I had been unwilling to take any action toward change.

"I was sober for about six months before I began to allow myself to really feel again. Suddenly, my sorrow, built up over all those years, poured out, and I shed many tears. It was not an easy time, but it was a necessary one. As time went by, I slowly began to put my life back together. I saw a counselor, cleared up my debts, reestablished myself at work, and began to take better care of my children.

"Although much of my story is painful, I believe if I am willing to be honest with myself and work for change, my life will continue to improve. My ordeal was long and hard, but now I stand tall for the first time. And for the first time in my life, I am taking care of myself, and feeling just fine on my own."

Demanding and Expecting Unconditional Love

The only time we really needed unconditional love was when we were infants. Unable to love, nurture, or protect ourselves, we needed care from others to keep us alive and growing.

It is perfectly all right for adults to want and to receive unconditional love, but to demand it is an unhealthy, unrealistic expectation. Why should someone grant you what you either didn't receive as a child or what you now are unwilling to grant to yourself? In addictive love we may refuse to love ourselves unconditionally and rage or weep when others fail to love us in that way.

❧   ❧   ❧

Dorothy, who sought therapy for chronic depression, appeared to be a demanding, whiny, angry young woman. Her need for love and approval from me, her counselor, seemed insatiable. She was angry that she had to pay for therapy; she was angry that the sessions weren't longer. "After all, isn't it my right to be loved?" she would ask. Her unspoken message to me was, "My parents didn't love me like I deserved to be loved, so you'd better!" I told Dorothy I was sorry she hadn't received the positive, unconditional love she had a right to as an infant, but I could not and would not make up for that loss. In reality, she no longer needed that unconditional love to live and thrive. In fact, when she made demands for unconditional love, I felt compelled to pull back from her rather than come close. And if I, her therapist, felt this way, how might others in her life feel? Dorothy acknowledged that her love relationships had been disastrous. Her insatiable neediness alternating with rageful demands to be the central figure in her partner's life resulted in two failed marriages marked by verbal and physical abuse. Her current marriage was also on dangerously thin ice. Her husband, a passive man filled with insecurities himself, would attempt to please Dorothy any way he could. Rarely satisfied, Dorothy would often verbally demean him. The words touched the inner core of his insecurity and suggested to him that he was not enough. He was very close to leaping out of the relationship to keep from striking back. Both Dorothy and her husband needed to learn to love themselves unconditionally and to place healthy conditions on their behaviors if the abuse was to stop. Paradoxically, this would also allow the deeper goodness of each person to be expressed and unconditionally affirmed by the other.

Refusing or Abusing Commitment

Addictive love often appears to be antidependent, to exhibit a clear refusal of commitment. In reality, this antidependency is the flip side of dependency. Our need to belong is real. People who say, "I'll do my thing and you do yours, and if we meet, so be it" promote a false independence.

I've discovered that most people who exalt their independence harbor many unfulfilled dependency needs. They've learned to avoid pain and fear by becoming self-sufficient. Control is important to them; when they were children, they often felt one or both parents were attempting to overpower them or each other. Paradoxically, those control-obsessed parents failed to meet basic developmental needs in the child, and often the child's response was, "No, I won't, and you can't make me!" or, "I'm okay; you're not!" These were important ways the child maintained a sense of personal power and dignity in an uneasy, unhealthy situation.

On the other hand, when children have weak, ineffective parents, the results can be similar. The children are forced to take care of themselves rather than entrust dependency to others. However, this self-promise to be completely independent makes it difficult to commit to a mature love relationship. It is not uncommon for an antidependent stance to turn into an abuse of commitment. A "you owe me" or "I own you" attitude has led to many of the unthinkable domestic abuse stories we hear about daily. Antidependence is pseudoindependence. Healthy independence assumes that one has had a healthy dependency relationship as a child.

Looking to Others for Affirmation and Worth

Very few people love themselves without reservation, yet everyone wants to be loved that way. Like young children, we search the world for people who will love us totally, and when a love affair ends, our self-esteem wanes. As mentioned earlier, it is normal to feel grief after a loss, but when a relationship ends or is floundering, it is unhealthy to connect this loss with a loss of personal value and self-esteem.

꙳   ꙳   ꙳

Judith, who had very low self-esteem, wrote the following letter from her addictive self to her healthy self to describe the unconscious motivation for her many bad habits.

"Judith, the reason why you are eating, smoking, and drinking so much is obvious. What else can you do? Behind your defenses is an empty shell, absolutely nothing. There is not a Judith. Your house, your job, your family, your car, your furniture, your plants, your clothes are all things that can be removed. You needed to think all these things were you, but you know better now. There is no you. You have no core; it's dead if it was ever there at all. I don't think you exist. The only times you felt like you existed were when you had someone to love you or you belonged to someone. And you don't have someone now. So you smoke, eat, and drink—at least they're something to help you feel alive."

꙳   ꙳   ꙳

People like Judith need to realize that it is their choice to enhance their lives. Most of us can be far happier and feel more fulfilled. Our stumbling block is our belief that someone else will do it for us. We overlook our ability to choose to develop ourselves. We not only can make our own choices, we can create our own chances.

Fearing Abandonment When Routinely Separated

Pathological aloneness is characterized by chronic panic, anger, despair, and emptiness; it differs from mature aloneness, which is a healthy wistfulness for an absent lover. Love addicts are unable to sustain comfortable memories of the beloved, and fear of abandonment often accompanies even the most routine separation. The addictive lover has trouble trusting the other person will return. This phenomenon seems to be the result of having missed an important developmental lesson in childhood. It is essential that infants trust in the permanence of their parents. As they do, they begin to comfort themselves with the memory of parental love during the parents' absence, trusting they can have it again. When children learn to distrust that inevitable return, they are unable to call on pleasant memories to sustain them during parental absences. As adults they may have trouble trusting their partners unless the partners are always in their sight.

෨෪ ෨෪ ෨෪

As a child, Jean was emotionally neglected by her parents. They seldom responded to her needs, and they often were physically abusive toward her. In therapy, Jean, an unusually hesitant and dependent young woman, took in positive messages about self-esteem and autonomy, but she was unable to trust and use those messages outside of therapy. Outside of my presence, Jean panicked and feared I would leave her and that her fragile new self-affirmation would vanish.

Jean needed to learn to trust her memory and to use the lessons from her therapy in her daily life. At first, she had to work hard at this, restating and revisualizing our discussions to recapture the good feeling she had about them. She learned we have the capacity to recall both pleasant and unpleasant feelings and memories, and that we can control that process. I could not put anything new into Jean, but only affirm what was already there and encourage her to develop self-worth.

Re-creating Familiar, Negative Feelings

Another prominent feature of addictive love is the recurrence of feelings like emptiness, excitement, depression, guilt, rejection, anxiety, self-righteous anger, and low self-esteem. These recurring feelings generally are the result of psychological games played out by dependent lovers. People generally have their own favorite set of feelings supported by unconscious myths about themselves, others, and life. Such feelings interfere with meeting psychological needs and make intimacy difficult.

Carla's favorite bad feeling was sadness. Ken's favorite bad feelings were rejection and self-righteous anger. Each knew how to get their bad feelings to pay off. Carla and Ken worked together and frequently met after work for drinks with other co-workers. Carla was flirtatious, and Ken responded. One night he invited her to his home for dinner. Carla only intended to be Ken's friend, and Ken believed her behavior indicated she was willing to engage in sex with him. When Ken made unwanted advances to Carla and she told him she wasn't interested, he felt rejected and ashamed, and he self-righteously lashed out at her. Carla felt misunderstood and burst into tears.

Desiring, Yet Fearing, Closeness

A great paradox of dependent love is that we really do want to love and be loved, but our addictive selves fear closeness. As we've said all along, addictive love is grounded in fear: fear of rejection, fear of pain, fear of losing control, fear of loss of self or loss of life, and fear of joy. And addictive love's intent is to avoid what we fear.

As a child who observed her parents' miserable, quarrelsome marriage, Nancy made a vow to herself to be cautious in love—in fact, to avoid it altogether. Such a vow is impossible for a normal person to keep, and Nancy fell in love while still a young woman. She deeply committed herself to a man who, without warning, broke off their engagement shortly before they were to be married. Nancy's pain ran doubly deep because she had broken the vow to herself. Her experience of being jilted confirmed her unconscious conviction that love inevitably led to pain. Unknowingly, she renewed and amplified that vow.

Several years later, she fell in love again. In spite of her deep affection for her new lover, she was unable to fully let go of herself in an emotionally committed or sexual way. Whenever she found herself opening up to intimacy, she felt fearful, guilty, and angry with herself.

Careful exploration of her feelings helped her discover her unconscious vow to stay free of risky love. She was able to see the futility of
such a vow, and Nancy eventually affirmed a willingness to take risks
in love—even though pain might be involved.

⅋ ⅋ ⅋

We all lose something or someone at some point, and we feel hurt.
People may try to control us and diminish our freedom, and we feel
frightened. We even fear joy because it might end. In many instances,
we are more content with being emotionless than we are with emotional highs or lows. Joy can be confusing to those who are unaccus-
tomed to it.

⅋ ⅋ ⅋

Pam had been in therapy for some time for severe depression. She
was ready to leave counseling because her self-esteem was high, her
relationship with her husband was solid, and she felt personal satisfaction for the first time in her life. One night she called me to tell me
not that her depression had returned, but that she felt very happy
and excited. In fact, she said, often she felt so ecstatic that she panicked; she didn't know if she could stand such an extended high, and
she felt almost frightened. I assured her that she could handle it, and
there were many ways in which she could channel her new energy
and self-confidence.

Attempting to "Fix" Others' Feelings

Perhaps the most pronounced characteristic of addictive love is this
unwritten rule: "You take care of my feelings, and I'll take care of
yours. You make me feel whole and good, and I'll do the same for
you."

Taking care of another adult's feelings is very different from caring about someone. The first assumes a person can read another's
mind, know another's needs, and "fix" the other's ill feelings. Such an
assumption makes one lover responsible for the other's well-being.

But true caring about someone means, "I care about what you

feel; I'm here to lend support although I do not have the power to make your pain go away or to help you feel complete in yourself." The first belief system is based on fear and guilt, the second on compassion and realism.

How often we expect others to read our minds and know what we want! "You should know; you've lived with me long enough," we say. How often we assume the other knows what we want, even though we've never asked for it. Maybe the other *does* know sometimes, or can guess correctly, but we will get more from our relationships by learning to read our own wants and needs, and then asking in ways that our partners are most likely to hear. We must ask clearly and with consideration for the other's position.

֍ ֍ ֍

When Stan's marriage began to fail, he entered therapy with his wife, Pat. He had a hard time understanding why things weren't working out; after all, he was doing all the "right" things. He was a good, loyal husband; he liked to please his wife. He worked hard; he was strong and didn't demand much, and he provided a lovely home for his family. Pat, however, was unhappy because of poor communication, a feeling of being smothered by Stan, and because of Stan's frequent, seemingly unprovoked, angry outbursts.

An even more complex problem was that Stan didn't know how to ask for what he needed and wanted. He had to relearn what he had known as a child—that his feelings offered clues to what he needed, and it was his responsibility to let others know what that was.

The Three P's: Projection, Personalizing, Power Plays

Addictive love is heaped with denial. Denial is fertile ground for the "three P's", the three cardinal sins of dysfunctional relationships: projection, personalizing, and power plays. The Funk & Wagnalls definition of *projection* is "to throw or forward into space or upon a surface as an image or shadow." Metaphorically, this definition accurately describes psychological projection. *Projection* means shifting blame onto another, or perceiving a quality or characteristic in someone else that one denies or does not wish to claim in oneself. It is the projection of one's shadow self, in Jungian terminology, onto others. *Personalizing* refers to those instances when we internalize the projections others make onto us, accepting them as truths about ourselves. It also refers to the times we "take personally" what others say and do even when they are not projecting onto us.

The first step in the dance of projection, personalizing, and power plays occurred in childhood. When others were too fragile, too unaware, or too afraid to vent their pent-up feelings, they took the shadow side of their own personalities and placed them on us. They saw in us, or attributed to us, what they denied in themselves. And it all happened before we knew what hit us. We were not perfect enough, caring enough, successful enough. We were sick, unappreciative, wrong, crazy, stupid, too sensitive, too angry, or too seductive. Not having the ability to stand up for ourselves or in a misguided attempt at being loyal to those we loved, we absorbed the projections of others and, as most children would, concluded, "You are probably right."

The second step of the dance occurred when we personalized the words and actions directed toward us. The result was a fundamental relational inequity: We were the "problem" and became the victims of their inadequacies. This inequality began for us an ongoing struggle for personal power and integrity.

Power plays, which will be discussed at some length in chapter 5, were the third step of the dance. Power plays are manipulative behaviors designed to maintain inequality in a relationship; they ensure that a person is either "one-up" or "one-down" with another person. Power plays are habits of relating that can become a way of life. If when we were children our adult role models taught us that power and love were commodities, something we could earn by playing certain designated roles or performing specific behaviors, we are likely to engage in power plays. Subtle or not so subtle, consciously devised or completely unconscious, power plays are usually hostile in nature and are always covert. In essence, they are schemes to get another to behave in ways we think will bring us inner satisfaction. Slowly, this pattern of behavior causes us to lose sight of who we really are. The dance becomes a way of life.

Christine's story illustrates several of these dynamics. As a child, she knew what she needed emotionally—warmth, attention, affection—and asked for it in direct ways. When others failed to respond, she personalized the lack of response and, little by little, her self-esteem eroded. Consequently, as an adult she looked to others to define who she was, what she was to do or not do, what feelings she was to express, and how successful her life would be. And, though she was criticized for acting as though she were powerless, her friends and family actually supported her acquiescence in covert ways since by doing so, they could maintain their one-up position and the illusion of power and control.

⁂ ⁂ ⁂

"Well, here I sit and sit and sit. The big question is always, Where do I start? At the beginning is the best, I guess. When I first went to therapy, my husband had had his second heart attack and I relapsed into serious drinking. I was becoming more depressed and knew that if I didn't get some additional support that I would be in trouble. My addictions were booze and staying stuck. I was stuck in a business I wanted out of. I felt stuck in my marriage of twenty-eight years, and I was stuck spiritually. *Stuck* meaning 'no growth.' After several months of therapy, learning about myself, about human psychological development in general, and discovering ways of recognizing my personal 'truths,' I came to a point where I truly experienced a major shift in my relationships. It happened through a series of events precipitated by therapy, a visit to a good friend, and a repeat dream in which I was able to clearly interpret the message of a life experience.

"My visit with my friend Gina was confrontational. She cut to the truth of the matter without mincing a word. She berated me for not having the courage to leave my husband at home and visit her whether he wanted me to visit her or not. She told me she thought my self-esteem must be terribly low, that if I really wanted to spend time with her as a friend, I would have showed up no matter what. I was able to sit and listen to her without personalizing her attacks or projecting my shortcoming onto her. She seemed intent on initiating a power struggle, but I didn't take the bait. In the past I would have experienced fear in a situation like that, and all the accompanying flight symptoms—sweating, rapid heart beat, tears—and would have done anything to get out of there. Instead, I listened intently, almost wanting to hear more, just in order to learn more about my behavior and how she interpreted it. I checked out the information internally to see what I thought was true and what was not.

"Less than two days later, I experienced a vivid dream, one which I'd had many times before and which always ended in exasperation and terror. As a young child, my bedroom was located in an area behind my parents' tavern at a fishing resort. In my dream, people of all ages were coming in and out of my room without knocking. They were loud, drunk, and scary. In the dream, I got very irritated and went out into the bar and attempted to kick people out. Closing time was coming up and I had to go to school the next day. While I was doing this, my sister was in my room rummaging through my clothes deciding which ones she would wear the next day. My father and his friends played the jukebox as loud as it would play. Girls that I had made friends with during the summer were laughing, drinking, and having fun. No matter what I did or said no one paid any attention to my pleas. Every time I got one or two of them out of the bar, several more entered. I woke from the dream feeling exhausted, ineffective, frustrated.

"I began to enter a downward spiral that before had led to a deep depression. I caught myself and decided to try something I was learning in therapy. I got up and wrote down the dream. I went back into the dream, consciously, as my adult self. I brought the night bartender into the dream and, as a grown-up, I told her to clean up the bar and get all of the patrons out by closing. Then I went into little Christine's bedroom, picked her up and held her. I told her that I loved her very much and that she had every right to feel as badly as she did. I told her that these people were rude, drunk, and suffered from a sickness that made them do things they should not be doing. I told her that I would make sure that no one ever came into her room again without her permission. They would be instructed to knock first and ask her if it was okay to come in. She deserved her privacy as much as anyone else. I stayed with her until she stopped crying and fell asleep.

"What I learned from the dream was that as a child my boundaries had been severely violated to the point that I felt I had no rights. Even when I put up a fuss nothing changed. I learned very early to put up with these intrusions because I believed there wasn't anything I could do about it. I can remember my mother saying to me, 'Can't you be more pleasant?' Being a good girl under the most adverse circumstances became my imprint, and it followed me to my adult life. I had been unable to take a stand in any situation where there might be a chance that someone would tell me 'no.' I chronically looked to someone else for permission to do what I wanted to do. This someone else was my father early in life, my husband later, and my best friend, even now.

"Within three weeks, time and with what I learned in therapy, I was able to move beyond my normal passive patterns, past the feeling of being frozen, beyond the dream that left me feeling helpless and afraid.

"I'm learning that through knowledge and recognition something changes in your heart. When the truth of what you hear and what you experience finally settles in your heart, it becomes your truth. Once something becomes your truth, it speaks to your soul and there is nothing except more knowledge and experience that can change it. And this was when I could truly thank God for helping me stay with the pain and wait for the results. My goal is to live my life without having to seek anyone else's approval, to live my life according to my truth, and to have approval stem from my accomplishments, my experiences, and what I give to my relationships."

Power Plays

When love is without power, we take care of others at our own expense. When power is without love, we hurt, injure, and abuse others—ultimately at our own expense.

Loving Me, Loving You

Power

One of the most pronounced features of overly dependent, unhealthy relationships is the use of power plays to gain a misguided sense of control over a partner. As mentioned in chapter 4, power plays are manipulative behaviors that keep two people relating on an unequal basis. Learning to recognize such behavior is a step toward purging it from our relationships or avoiding relationships based on power plays.

The word power is used in many ways. In regard to the search for love and interdependence, the power we strive for springs from self-esteem (personal potency), not from control over others.

The myth underlying power plays is: there is not enough power for two; one person must maintain control. The myth is based on the belief that people with power have control, and they can get what they want and need. Without such control, life seems tenuous and uncertain. And, of course, we all want to feel certain! Competition for the mysterious thing called "control" is often fierce, as is evident in wars. Often, we don't even know what we want to control. Moreover, power players—aptly called "controllers"—mistakenly believe that other people provide or take away their personal potency. Where do such beliefs come from?

The Beginnings of Power Plays

As children, we started to fight for power at about age two, when we were told by our parents it was time to stop being the center of the universe, and cooperation with "the big people" was now necessary. We could remember, we could talk, and we could act in socially cooperative ways. If we didn't cooperate, we were often punished or rejected. In this situation, children have three options: they may rebel, overadapt, or cooperate.

Rebels say, "No, I won't go along, and you can't make me," and fight to have their own way. We've all seen children attempt to overpower and often win over a parent by saying no, holding out, and throwing temper tantrums.

Overadapters are often overpowered by a parent. They may feel they are being swallowed up, that their freedom is being stripped away. They may feel grief and fear because their behavior and freedom of choice are being suppressed, not directed. And so they adapt and withhold anger.

Those children who are guided to cooperate and to recognize that others have needs slowly learn cooperation, and growing up can be a joy. Power sharing and yielding, the basis of healthy love, become normal parts of life.

There was no need to overpower our parents, nor did they need to overpower us with directives, bribes, threats, demands, and physical punishment. Parents and children alike can be powerful in their own ways, and in sharing power, they construct bridges of communication, support, and love. That is normal development.

Every two- or three-year-old child moves through the rebellious stage. Some emerge with few emotional scars, though everyone I have met has some problems with trying to control others. The roots of adult power players' behavior often can be traced back into childhood. There are many ways in which children can be helped through this difficult time, even taught that power need not be something one person has at another's expense.

꒰ꇰ ꒰ꇰ ꒰ꇰ

When my daughter, Heidi, was three, she toddled into the kitchen where I was washing dishes and thinking about the chores I had to complete that evening. "Mommy, read me a story," Heidi said, tugging on my skirt. I looked down, grimacing at the toys scattered across the floor of the kitchen and living room. I thought, Well, I've got time to either read her a story or pick up those toys.

I started to say, "Go pick up your toys and then we'll talk about a story," but I suddenly stopped, realizing I would be issuing an irritated order. Instead, I said: "Heidi, I only have time to do one thing; read to you or pick up all those toys. Why don't you decide which I should do?"

I had given the child a choice, and Heidi was startled. She had no cause for disappointment or a temper tantrum, because it was her choice. And she chose: she ran to pick up the toys herself, then returned for the one thing I had time for—reading the story. Getting her to think and choose affirmed her personal power.

꒰ꇰ ꒰ꇰ ꒰ꇰ

The transition from childish omnipotence to power sharing seems to be something we all struggle with in childhood and adolescence, even in adult life. Confusion over the uses of power is evident in unhealthy, uneasy adult relationships. What are some of the power plays that sabotage adult love relationships?

Twenty-Three Power Plays

1. Giving advice but not accepting it
2. Having difficulty in reaching out and in asking for support and love
3. Giving orders; demanding and expecting much from others
4. Trying to "get even" or to diminish the self-esteem or power of others
5. Being judgmental; put-downs that sabotage others' success; faultfinding; persecuting; punishing

6. Holding out on others; not giving what others want or need
7. Making, then breaking, promises; causing others to trust us and then betraying the trust
8. Smothering, overnurturing others
9. Patronizing, condescending treatment of others that sets one partner up as superior, the other as inferior; intimidation
10. Making decisions for others; discounting others' abilities to solve problems
11. Putting others in no-win situations
12. Attempting to change others (and unwillingness to change self)
13. Attacking others when they are most vulnerable
14. Showing an antidependent attitude: "I don't need you"
15. Using bullying, bribing behavior; using threats
16. Showing bitterness, or self-righteous anger; holding grudges
17. Abusing others verbally, emotionally, sexually, or physically
18. Being aggressive and defining it as assertiveness
19. Needing to win or be right
20. Resisting stubbornly or being set in one's own way
21. Having difficulty admitting mistakes or saying "I'm sorry"
22. Giving indirect, evasive answers to questions
23. Defending any of the above behaviors

To feel powerful, one person must overwhelm and control another; the power player has difficulty sharing power for fear of being overpowered. Such a person is unconsciously saying, "I fear I'm powerless and need others to control so that I may be powerful." This false belief suggests another person is in charge of our personal potency, and we need to control the other person in order to be secure and strong.

The power player struggles to keep others in the position of a victim so they can be rescued or persecuted. Such melodramatics are not the essence of true personal power, but of dependency; they are very unhealthy. Ultimately, power plays are the cause of much unhappiness.

Power playing is not easily given up, for it masks unconscious and often suppressed fears. In each incidence where I have explored the roots of a client's need to control another person, I've found a traumatic experience or imagined threat that led him or her to interpret loss of control as a loss of self, which is a dangerous and terrifying idea. Or, perhaps, the client had been allowed to overpower his or her parents, and thus developed a belief that, "I am more powerful than you and I can get my own way."

"Besides," reasoned one power player, "being powerful feels much better, so why give up that behavior?" They fail to recognize that these positions are unstable and unhealthy, and are based on false beliefs. People attempting to control others can avoid dealing with their own private fears, insecurities, and doubts because they always have someone else who is "less okay" to focus on. Keep in mind that power players and their victims both play the game. The victim sees benefits too. Cooperating keeps the other person around, helps the victim avoid looking at his or her own fear, keeps life predictable, and provides recognition, stimulation, and a sense of security. Perhaps most important is that it validates the inner beliefs that the victim has carried for years: "Power does not belong to me"; "I can get what I need by being still"; "Power is scary"; "I won't get hurt if I cooperate"; "If I am powerful, people will leave me"; "I'm not important enough, smart enough, strong enough to speak up."

Because we may have designed our power plays in childhood to protect us from harm, they are deeply embedded behaviors, and our resistance to giving them up will be very great.

Power players who strive to maintain the one-up position seldom reach out for help or indicate they want to change. This is largely due to their domination by delusion and denial, as well as their belief that they are better than others. Generally, they are forced into therapy or change when they experience a trauma—such as a partner's threat to leave. Even then, their goal may be to regain control over the rebellious partner. At this point, the partner usually is no longer willing to be a victim. Sometimes, the partner may be angry and may even be competing for the dominating position. Neither person will be ready to give up power playing until the insecurities that motivate them have been explored.

A crucial characteristic of dependent love is the presence of power plays when one partner gains a misguided sense of control over the other. Manipulative or controlling behaviors are intended to keep the partners in a one-up, one-down situation. To feel powerful, one person overwhelms the other. The controller has difficulty sharing power for fear of being overpowered, and can avoid dealing with private fears, insecurities, and doubts by focusing on someone who is "less okay." Without such control, life feels fragile and uncertain. Power players often interpret loss of control as a loss of self. This fallacy, based on the idea that power is scarce, suggests that another person is in charge of our personal potency.

❧   ❧   ❧

Pete, who was seeking help for his depression and low self-esteem, wrote the following letter to himself from the side of him that needed to control.

"You've always had a strong ego and been so self-sufficient, and now you are thinking of turning all that over to another person who will cause you to lose control. You don't really want this, do you? I've tried to protect you in a thousand ways. Maybe you forgot how I stuck with you and wouldn't let others get close to you. I've kept you alone and in complete control. You are so intelligent and above others who try to help. You don't need them because you can figure it out for yourself. It's worked quite well all these years, right?

"Why you want to admit defeat or the need for help mystifies me. You can be in the driver's seat. The powerful ones are the ones in control; this is where you want to be and stay. Most of your problems stem from others trying to thwart you. Push them out of the way and things will really start happening for you."

🙦 🙦 🙦

Pete listed all the ways he would attempt to con me in therapy.

1. Laugh or smile my hurt feelings away
2. Dominate the conversation
3. Get her to feel sorry for me
4. Become defensive when things get touchy
5. Convince her others are to blame
6. Keep the sessions nonserious
7. Intellectualize
8. Appear flexible
9. Overcooperate
10. Find her soft part and capitalize on it
11. Find out what pain she has suffered and commiserate
12. Try to become emotionally involved
13. Try to induce self-doubt
14. Question her motive for helping
15. Talk around the subject at hand

Pete was using these cons to reinforce his need to control. With the help of therapy, he later learned that his personal power did not come at another's expense. Our personal power comes from within; there is no need to win control over another. With self-confidence, we let go of the need for power and control.[1]

Options

Once we identify the power plays sabotaging our relationships, we have three options.

First, we could cooperate and respond passively as a victim, agreeing to forfeit our own potency and to accept our one-down submissive position. It is easy and familiar, even though addictive. Needless to say, this is no way to live fully, although many people do it. These people usually end up with the feelings the other person is trying to avoid—shame, guilt, inadequacy, and fear. "She overpowered me," "He took my power away," and, "I'm powerless when it comes to her seductions" are delusions that suggest that personal power is a commodity controlled by others rather than being our life energy.

Second, we could seek the one-up power position, but we may become snared in a competitive addictive relationship. In this case, two antidependent people vie for the power position, living in constant conflict as each tries to overwhelm the other with creative and destructive power-play tactics. "I'm giving you back your power" and "I'm taking my power back" are statements that reinforce the belief that power is an item controlled by another. Unfortunately, most relationships alternate between options one and two, seesawing through life.

However, there's a third, much happier option—to respond from an affirmative position that acknowledges equal personal power. In this position we are saying, "We are both okay and personally powerful. Sometimes, your behavior is not acceptable to me." We acknowledge that, "I acted as though I gave her my power," "I acted as though he owned me," or, "She acted as though she had power over me." Such ownership is empowering.

It is a matter of consciously reclaiming our power over our own lives. When our lives become unmanageable because of a toxic attachment, we can either work to change the relationship or remove ourselves from the attachment. The slogan "Let go and let God" does not suggest that we passively wait for intercession or deny our own personal power. On the contrary, it suggests power sharing, doing what we can do in a situation and then letting go.

When we choose this option, it is important to recognize how power plays have victimized both players, and to work to nurture a new sense of personal power and dignity for both.

Listed here are things we must do if we are to withdraw from power plays.

1. Acknowledge that power plays are real
2. Take an inventory of the power plays we most often use
3. Learn to identify our personal cues: feeling confused, trapped, guilty, uncomfortable, threatened, competitive; doubting ourselves; making sarcastic rebuffs; being defensive; projecting blame; avoiding our partners; giving evasive responses

4. Examine our personal negative beliefs that are supporting power plays and change them
5. Detach ourselves; believe we are equals

We win by learning an internal process: how to live with ourselves. If we have a sense of confidence, we no longer need to "win" at another's expense.

The Goal: Mutual Respect

You may find that when an argument stems from the power-seeking behavior of a partner, the less you say in response to verbal challenges, the better. The urge to defend or to agree can lead you directly back into addictive behavior. Short, one-word responses are most effective in order to stay detached from power competition. Or, you may choose to state your position: "When you ___(Action)___, I feel ___(Feeling)___." You are responding from a position of equal personal power. Make the statement at a time you are most likely to be heard, not when you are angry or in the midst of an argument. The following is an example of a couple moving toward a healthier relationship based on each partner's equal personal power.

⋙ ⋙ ⋙

Jennifer and Brad had a potentially good relationship. But Brad was obsessed with his role as rescuer and adviser to many people— the role of one trying to hold power over others. Brad had many "victims" demanding his time and energy, people Jennifer called "hangers-on," and not true friends. Though Brad often complained that these people ate up his time, he could not say no to them.

Jennifer often felt neglected, but for several years she said little, always hoping the situation would change. Her style, one she had learned from her family, was to say nothing and feel bad. Because she had not experienced power sharing in her family, her fear of confronting Brad, possibly causing him to grow angry and reject her, was very real.

When she finally gathered the courage to confront him, she did so with great feeling and honesty. She told Brad she was no longer willing to postpone her own needs for those of his acquaintances. She said, "When you cancel our weekend plans because a friend wants you to help him move, I feel unimportant, hurt, and very angry." She had begun to recognize that her behavior was a pattern carried over from childhood, when she had often bowed to the needs of others in her family. She no longer wanted to do this.

At first, Brad listened sympathetically; later, he verbally attacked Jennifer, accusing her of manipulating him with tears and trying to control their relationship. To regain his equilibrium, Brad began to criticize her, to withhold affection from her, and to lecture her on how their marriage should and would be from then on.

Jennifer knew she could comply, stand and affirm her personal dignity, or leave the marriage. Fortunately, she was strong enough to recognize that although Brad's behavior hurt her, it stemmed from his fear of losing control and being hurt himself. Determined not to remain a victim, Jennifer maintained detachment and did not take his criticism personally.

When an opportune time arose, she told Brad how his behavior affected her, although she knew she could not realistically expect to change him and that changing lifelong patterns would not be easy. She also made it clear she wanted a healthy marriage in which both of them could contribute their own thoughts, feelings, and ways of doing things as equals without fear of reprisal. Jennifer hoped such an ideal could be achieved; if it couldn't, she said, she would have no choice but to consider how or if she would remain in this relationship.

Fortunately, both Jennifer and Brad now are working to achieve a stronger, freer relationship. It hasn't been easy for them, but mutual respect has allowed them to move from a controlling, addictive relationship to one that supports—yet frees—them both. There are fewer power plays, and they are better for that—individually and as a couple.

☙ ☙ ☙

I continue to be amazed at how frequently people begin getting what they want and need in relationships when they are willing to give up the need to control. Perhaps they can do this because one partner senses that the other's power lies confidently within and, in awe and respect, is moved to reach out and give. Or, perhaps, they discover that control over others is an illusion and the answer is in letting go. In a storm, it is the tree that bends with the wind that survives to grow tall.

Healthy Belonging

Love one another, but make not a bond of love:
Let it rather be a moving sea between the shores of your
*   souls.*
Fill each other's cup but drink not from one cup.
Give one another of your bread but eat not from the same
*   loaf.*
Sing and dance together and be joyous, but let each one of
*   you be alone,*
Even as the strings of a lute are alone though they quiver
*   with the same music.*
Give your hearts, but not into each other's keeping.
For only the hand of Life can contain your hearts.
And stand together yet not too near together:
For the pillars of the temple stand apart,
And the oak tree and the cypress grow not in each other's
*   shadow.*

KAHLIL GIBRAN, The Prophet[1]

Our Need for Others

If you recognize symptoms of love addiction or unhealthy dependency in yourself or your relationship, you aren't alone. In our struggle to end our sense of isolation, pain, and irrelevancy, we often find ourselves snared in a web of needfulness.

We do need other people. We need to love and to share love in order to bloom to our fullest. As Erich Fromm said, "The affirmation of one's own life, happiness, growth, freedom, is rooted in one's capacity to love—in care, respect, responsibility, and knowledge."[2] We turn now from a diagnosis of the ills that can plague a relationship to focus on the signs of healthy love.

We are the most highly evolved species on the planet. We continue to evolve. In our evolution, there is developing a spiritual awareness that we are linked with other people in a very profound way. Each individual's uniqueness contributes to the greater whole of humanity.

If we think of ourselves as individual energy systems, we realize we can choose to inhibit our energy, or use it in either destructive or constructive ways. Even love can be a form of energy that we suppress or exercise. Our scientists have discovered the atom and its component parts. They now strive to categorize the substance that causes the particles of the atom to adhere together. Some teachers of physics suggest that love is also a tangible force, a power. This concept views love as a power as real as electricity, a divine mortar that cements the universe together—an electromagnetic force that draws the particles of the atoms together and takes form. It makes sense to know more about *how* we love—whether it is dependent love aimed at ego enhancement and need fulfillment, or a mature love that has evolved over time.

True love's characteristics are the opposites of those that describe addictive relationships. Let's take a look at them.

The Characteristics of Healthy Belonging

People in healthy relationships have the following characteristics. Generally, they

1. allow for individuality
2. experience both oneness with and separateness from others
3. bring out the best qualities in themselves and others
4. accept endings
5. experience openness to change and exploration

6. invite growth in others
7. experience true intimacy
8. feel the freedom to ask honestly for what they want
9. experience giving and receiving in the same way
10. avoid attempts to change or control others
11. encourage self-sufficiency of others
12. accept limitations of themselves and others
13. learn not to seek unconditional love
14. accept and respect commitment
15. have high self-esteem
16. trust their memory of their beloved ones; enjoy solitude
17. express feelings spontaneously
18. welcome closeness; risk vulnerability
19. care with detachment
20. affirm equality and personal power of themselves and others

Now, let's consider these characteristics in more detail.

Allowing for Individuality

In addictive love, we feel we are being consumed, while healthy love allows for individuality. A healthy relationship allows the lovers to change and grow in separate ways without one lover feeling threatened. Such freedom is possible because of the mature lover's respect and trust for a partner. Individual thoughts and feelings are accepted, not suppressed. Body and mind can remain relaxed when differences and conflicts arise because differences are acceptable and resolution of conflicts is considered a part of normal, everyday life. The lovers don't feel they have to take care of each other's feelings, and they are self-directed enough not to panic when the beloved is mentally preoccupied elsewhere.

Experiencing Both Oneness with and Separateness from Others

Although mature lovers may describe their closeness as oneness, they also have a clear sense of being separate individuals. That is, *both oneness and separateness are experienced, and are not contradictory.* This allows for a state of euphoria denied addictive lovers, who are obsessed with the relationship at the expense of the self.

To master the experience of oneness and separateness, healthy boundaries are essential. Think of a boundary as a semipermeable sheath or membrane around you. Because it is semipermeable, it can let in what it needs or wants, and expel what it does not need or want. It can breathe! Though there is a clear line of demarcation, because of the permeability, love, power, and intuition can be exchanged with ease. Key to developing healthy boundaries is knowing our needs and limits and speaking about them to others respectfully.[3]

❧   ❧   ❧

Netty, a client of mine, was able to learn this truth and purge her obsessive dependency on her husband. First, she had to learn who she was and what she had to do in this life separate from others. Once she began to develop a sense of this, she was able to share her inner self with her husband in ways she had not been able to do earlier.

Netty had entered marriage counseling with Cliff, her husband of fifteen years who had recently undergone successful treatment for chemical dependency. After many group sessions, Netty announced that she was ready to leave therapy. She said she felt love for Cliff that she had not experienced before.

Netty, haunted by years of low self-esteem and fear of rejection, had tried to make her husband love her in a fashion that matched her ideal of romance and marriage. She insisted that he make up for the losses she had experienced as a child. Cliff did not respond. He, instead, put up a wall to protect himself. Netty's unrealistic demands widened the rift between them. Netty's ideal—like that of many people who think of their illusions as romantic—assumed an almost suffocating dependency on Cliff. From Cliff's perspective it felt as though Netty's boundaries were so lax that she defined herself by what he thought, felt, and did or didn't do. He also admitted that before going through treatment for chemical abuse he needed Netty to be dependent on him so she would support his sickness. Now that he was clearer on who he was, he felt repulsed by her dependency.

In therapy, Netty had learned she was a complete person in herself and that she did not *need* her husband to define her. But wanting him was a very different and much more gratifying emotion. This realization eased much of her frustration, anger, and fear of rejection; it allowed her to relax mentally, emotionally, and physically. With less stress, Netty was free to explore her own talents and dreams. Gradually, she began to understand that self-love results in healthy boundaries that free one to love others while allowing them their individuality. She developed her own identity. Cliff was invited to share her love. Under these conditions, two people could merge without losing their individuality. Cliff could let down his guard, and Netty could meet him as an equal.

Bringing Out the Best Qualities in Ourselves and Others

This is a rather subtle, but very visible and wonderful, aspect of mature love. In fact, it invites us to a higher quality of life, for it urges from our depths the highest human qualities: respect, patience, self-discipline, commitment, cooperation, generosity, and humility. Mature love isn't always easy, but it feels right in the final analysis. Mature love is for grown-ups, and achieving it is part of the process of growing up.

Accepting Endings

The death of a relationship is painful, but mature people have enough respect for themselves and their partners to cope when love is over. Mature people know how to let go of unsalvageable relationships, just as they are able to survive crises in healthy ones. Even in their grief, they do not doubt they will love again someday. We can survive pain, though there's no denying its power over us.

I've witnessed strong people break down and cry when they are sexually betrayed by a lover, even when they may themselves have cheated on their partners. Upon learning that his wife was having an affair, one man said to me, "I have never felt so much pain in all my life. I honestly don't know if I can live through it. The funny thing is, I never thought about love before all this happened. She was just

there, being my wife and helper, raising the kids. God, I feel terrible.
I never, ever want to go through this again."

The tragedy in his last sentence is that he was programming himself to never again be open to love. In order not to lose such vital
openness, a wounded lover must transcend the natural tendency to
react with anger, fear, jealousy, and panic. We have the power to sur-
mount pain and grief, and to once again forgive and love.

It sounds difficult, and it is. It takes one's spiritual side to over-
come the strong, self-destructive rule of pain and anger. In time, mature people are able to accept reality—even when it hurts—and move
on to the next chapter in their lives. They face up to problems and
sorrows in the healthiest, most rational way, even though it isn't easy.

The following story reveals an important fact: *single is sacred,
too*. Often, a person will remain in an intensely destructive relationship to avoid the pain of ending or the fear of failure. Though we
have a responsibility to honor commitments and do what we can do
to heal our half of the relationship, we must not be shamed into staying in relationships at all costs. Current political media hype often
suggests that we must endure abusive or empty relationships no
matter what. One infomercial is so bold as to declare that, just by
subscribing to its product, any relationship problem can be cured. In
addition, it suggests that a person should not trust the counsel of
anyone who has had more than one marriage. Such a proclamation
publicly shames people who are single, separated, or divorced, and
may go so far as to endorse staying in abusive and sometimes violent
relationships. In some corners of American culture, single parents
are considered inferior. (What this implies about the children of
these parents is material for an entire book!) Most important for our
discussion on the characteristics of healthy love, however, is that
these messages negate a tremendously valuable experience, that of
self-intimacy. Too often we jump from one relationship to the next
without stopping to say hello to ourselves. We must learn to differen-
tiate when a person leaves or stays in a relationship for the right reasons from when a person leaves or stays for the wrong reasons. There
is a difference. A healthy person knows when enough is enough,
when it is time to let go, and then is willing to accept the ending of

the relationship. Charlie offers a chapter from his life story that helps delineate some of these distinctions. Perhaps it will support what you have done or need to do.

≫ ≫ ≫

"We were in the same car pool that went to a company where we both worked. We were both ending brief unhappy initial marriages, hers to a closet alcoholic, mine to a woman who thought sex ended with the honeymoon. Passing the time together on a rainy Saturday, we ended up making love. Within four months we were married. That was twenty-six years ago.

"If I miss anything now, it's the early years of pregnancy and birth, building a house, planting an orchard, and raising a garden. I was the wage earner. She stayed home to be a full-time mother, jelly maker, and tomato canner.

"In the tenth year, she unexpectedly became pregnant and bore our third child. Frustrated in her mother role, and wanting professional satisfaction, she began a private business enterprise. I thought I was being supportive, but perhaps I was too insensitive emotionally. At any rate, I found out she was having an affair with a consultant she had met in the course of her daily business activities.

"I was too weak to confront her over the issue. Whenever I brought up our relationship problems, she responded with stares filled with cold rage, from which I turned away. I went into a deep depression. I dragged her along to a marriage therapist. He told me he had to work with me alone, as she was too brittle for therapy. I tried to follow his behavioral prescriptions, but I kept getting more depressed. Then came the day on which I decided to end my life. I was half an hour from carrying it out, when something moved inside me; for the first time I looked deep into my soul and found depths and strength there I'd had no idea existed. The depression slid away. I sought out her lover, confronted him, and threatened to ruin his career publicly if he didn't get out of our lives. He got out.

"As the next few years went by, these new strengths in me found expression in an ability to do spiritual healing. I trained with masters. I began a private practice. At age fifty-four I took an early retirement to do my new work full time. My wife was supportive initially but soon became afraid of my work because it was not sanctioned by our church. Her fear turned into rage when I ignored her demands to stop. She turned our youngest child against me, telling him to avoid knowing anything about my work.

"We went into marriage counseling again. The therapist was new and naïve and ineffective.

"My wife's rage kept escalating as she was unable to control me. She began demanding that I take her on extravagant vacations that were impossible with our income. She found more and more faults to blame me for. Then something happened that broke my passivity.

"I told her one morning that I would get home quite late because I would be going to the birthday party of a friend (someone she happened to dislike). She said she would go to bed and would see me the next morning. When I returned home from the party at 10:30 P.M., she was waiting for me, snarling, "Where have you been? You've never been this late before!" I realized that this was a setup to give her another justification to vent rage at me. That night I had a vivid dream of being tied down while she castrated me. The dream woke me up!

"I quietly began making arrangements to stay with friends. Then I confronted her, telling her my soul was dying in this relationship and I would be leaving for a few weeks to find out whether I wanted to come back. Within ten days she had borrowed $5,000 from a credit account I had neglected to close, rented a luxury apartment, and filed for divorce.

"So at age fifty-eight I am in divorce proceedings, financially impoverished, but more at peace than I ever remember being. I am surrounded by caring, supportive friends. I live day by day, and each day is new and beautiful."

Experiencing Openness to Change and Exploration

Life is a series of changes, yet many of us cling to familiar people and things, disregarding our inner desire to grow as individuals and in our relationships. Openness to change can be risky—it can even lead to breakups—but without it, a relationship will lose its vibrancy.

Often, one partner continues on a growth spiral while the other clings stubbornly to the familiar and seemingly safe. That may mean trouble.

Grant and Barbara met and fell in love when they were philosophy students in college. They were alive with the excitement of discovering and sharing new ideas and experiences. After they married, their lives slowly began to change—and then, suddenly, everything came to a standstill. Grant worked outside the home; Barbara was a homemaker. Their upper-middle-class lifestyle, so different from their college ideals, featured a hectic social life and a quest for material possessions. Grant embraced his role as provider, loyal company man, and consumer. Barbara acted as faithful companion and supporter of her husband's career.

They had been married for about twelve years when boredom and restlessness began to drive a wedge between them. Barbara, approaching middle age, entered graduate school and once again began to be moved by new ideas and experiences. She was eager to share it all with Grant, but to her bewilderment, he resisted her and belittled her schoolwork. Frightened, Barbara ceased talking to him about her experiences. Meanwhile, Grant had extramarital affairs and began to drink too much. It was clear they had drifted apart. Their relationship was devoid of warmth and excitement. At that point, recognizing that their marriage was in peril, they sought counseling.

At first, Grant and Barbara saw the problem as one of communication, but they found it was much more profound. Because they had neglected individual growth in favor of intense social involvement and competition for business and status, their spiritual sides had stagnated. They suffered from the strong but vague sense that something was missing. The results were Barbara's very real excitement when she began once again to nurture her creative side and Grant's frustrated search for stimulation and excitement in casual sex and frequent drunkenness. Through counseling, Grant and Barbara learned that without openness to change and exploration, a relationship is like a body that is never exercised—it loses flexibility and power; it weakens and may even die.

Inviting Growth in Others

Not only do mature people recognize that change is necessary, they know that true love urges and encourages growth in the other, including the development of other important relationships without feelings of jealousy.

I spoke recently with a very dear male friend. At that moment, he was my most important friend and I was his. We spoke about how this might change if we were lovers. We concluded that when sex is involved, other vital friendships can often cause jealousy. Though there may be little rational reason for jealousy, it is an enormous force in our emotional and biological makeups. It is deeply rooted in our biology—perhaps the result of our primal urges toward procreation and protection—and it is also something we learn. Jealousy is a natural emotion, but if we allow it to control us, we may cut off our own growth and that of our partner.

Personal development doesn't end at age eighteen; it continues until death. At midlife, we are confronted with a choice: stagnation or personal self-discovery that may lead to renewed growth. It is a time when many people feel confused and challenged. Because many people fear change, they may choose to stagnate intellectually and emotionally, and their other relationships suffer as a result. In *The Bridge Across Forever*, Richard Bach wrote: "Boredom between two people . . . doesn't come from being together physically. It comes from being apart mentally and spiritually."[4]

Experiencing True Intimacy

Because mature lovers are not shackled by childhood fears and inhibitions, their relationships feature true, intense intimacy. Fear of love's risks inhibits intimacy; trust and the willingness to take risks invite it. True love seems contradictory: those who are self-contained and independent are better able to deeply, tenderly love another. Because their love is not obsessive or dependent, they are free to be interdependent, complementing their partners. That is, those who are free as individuals also are free to love. It may look like a paradox, but if you think about it, it is not. Intimate love occurs only in an atmosphere of trust. As infants, we were willing to trust ourselves, others, and life. Thus, the inner child is always involved in our capacity to love intimately. In order to entrust ourselves to another, four qualities must be present—*reliability, openness, acceptance, and congruence.*

Whenever one of the trust qualities is missing, we experience distrust, and rightly so. Our intuitive selves are very quick to respond and begin defending us. In healthy love, a person can count on the other being there, can feel safe and accepted, can experience an openness to thoughts, feelings, and differences, and can experience consistency in the other. *Congruence* means that one's words and actions are consistent. When one's thoughts and actions are inconsistent, acknowledging it can make them congruent. Saying, "I love you" and not expressing it is incongruent. "I love you, but I have problems expressing love" acknowledges the incongruence and puts one back in a state of congruence.

In healthy belonging, partners work to create an atmosphere of trust, respect, and safety that sets the stage for intimacy. Relationships that permit us to be who we are nourish closeness and allow us to grow from conflict. Free to be imperfect, we can take risks that, paradoxically, encourage perfection. We are then more likely to stay in our relationships and learn the lessons that love relationships can teach us.

ॐ ॐ ॐ

Intimacy is profound when we fully trust. Penny was often scared and stayed away from people. When she didn't trust, she was told by various people in her life that she was the problem. I gave her the list of characteristics of trust and told her to look at which quality was missing in people she encountered. As she did this, she began realizing that her distrust was often well founded. As she learned to trust her perceptions, she had more confidence in herself and took more risks with intimacy. She found she could learn the difference between safe and unsafe people. She also learned no one is perfect and that healthy people were open to talking with her about their incongruence, making them believable and safe to be with.

Feeling the Freedom to Ask Honestly for What We Want

True love means being free to ask and to receive, as well as being willing to accept no for an answer at times. It can't be stressed enough that the ability to be honest—to say "no" when one means no—is essential in a relationship. In fact, one's "yes" cannot be trusted until one has also demonstrated the ability to say no.

One important way I determine a formerly dependent client's readiness to leave therapy is evidence of the ability to reach out to others, to ask clearly for help when it is needed, and to receive help from others. It is also necessary for people to let go of their desire for things that cannot realistically be obtained.

I work with couples who frequently expect others to be mind readers. They often say to each other, "You've lived with me long enough. You should know what I need by now!" That's a mistake. At times your partner does know what you need; at other times he or she can "read" you correctly, or may simply guess correctly. But most often it is best to negotiate, to talk about feelings and needs. Most of us are not mind readers, and even love can't make us clairvoyant!

ℑ№   ℑ№   ℑ№

With the help of therapy, Joan, a very hesitant, quiet woman of thirty-five, had accomplished many new things. She could talk honestly about her feelings and directly ask her lover, Clark, for what she wanted instead of expecting him to guess. One day she came to me feeling very sad and angry. "I did everything I was supposed to," she said. "I wanted Clark to do something for me and I asked him in a clear, gentle way. Do you know what he said? He said 'no'! He refused me."

Joan had done the right things, but she had made a common mistake: she thought if she asked in the right way, she'd get what she wanted. Although we often get what we want when we ask in a direct fashion, it is important to ask the right person at the right time, and even then accept that the person might not be in a position to help. Joan hadn't done that.

People often get into trouble when they *expect* to get what they need or want. Needing or wanting things is natural, but expecting or demanding to receive them only sets us up for disappointment. Healthy love is willing to let go, not of a partner, but the expectations. To be accepted by others, we should have an attitude of acceptance ourselves.

Often, we expect people to fit our ideal of expressing love. One person in a relationship may enjoy running errands for the other, while the other may be more sentimental and like to give flowers, cards, and gifts. If both partners are perceptive and mature, they'll know the method of giving is unique to the giver, and many forms of expressing love will be welcome. True lovers appreciate—even savor—such differences.

Experiencing Giving and Receiving in the Same Way

Nonegocentric love experiences giving and receiving similarly. Pleasure obtained in giving to the beloved is as intense as that gained in receiving from him or her. When one has made the marvelous leap from dependency to freer love, one can give more easily and with fewer expectations. Some people give to please; by so pleasing, they hope to receive in return. When this fails, they may get angry and say, "Well, forget you! I've given and given and it didn't do any good!"

Anger and frustration often mark a turning point for a giver who gives to get. At this point, a giver may quit such egocentric giving in frustration and begin to be more honest with a partner. A client's husband once called me and said, "Geez, I don't know about this therapy. My wife is driving me up a wall. She's angry all the time and refuses to do a thing for me." I said, "It's only a phase, and someday you'll understand."

Weeks later, he called me to say, "You were right. She's back to her old self." In truth, the woman, who had been "giving-to-get," wasn't back to her old self; she was very different. She was learning to give to her husband, to do things that pleased him, not because she expected anything in return, but because she truly loved him and was experiencing the joy of giving for its own sake. Her anger and frustration over the failure of giving-to-get had been a natural phase—one in which some relationships flounder. Giving from our essence is a profound experience that encourages us to expand our giving to others.

Avoiding Attempts to Change or Control Others

Mature love accepts the self and others as they are. One lover does not try to change or control the other. This does not assume that one partner likes everything about himself or herself or the other; he or she is, however, able to put dislikes into perspective. That is, the best romances are based on realism.

Though it may sound simple enough, one of the most difficult parts of love is learning to accept ourselves and others as we and they are. Life and relationships are filled with choices. If we choose to be with someone, accepting that person as is, that is real love. Attempting to change another is a symptom of addictive love. And as anyone who has ever tried knows, it never works. Healthy love yields to the other. People on a higher level of awareness feel misunderstood by others on a lower level because those others have not had enough experience. A five-year-old can know what it is like to be a three-year-old, but not vice versa. Addictive love pushes and pulls. Healthy love is compassionate.

Encouraging Self-Sufficiency of Others

Fromm writes: "The most important step is to learn to be alone with oneself without reading, listening to the radio, smoking, or drinking. . . . This ability is precisely a condition for the ability to love." Mature love occurs when we realize we are substantial alone, that we no longer need as we needed in infancy and childhood, that we have qualities within us that make us complete. In a healthy relationship, both individuals have a sense of self-esteem and well-being. They trust themselves and others; on a scale of zero to ten, they love themselves unconditionally—a ten!—without guilt. I believe we all have what it takes to love and respect ourselves that much.

Accepting Limitations of Ourselves and Others

True love involves a realistic appraisal of our limitations. It is important that we adjust our beliefs to what is real, rather than try to twist reality to fit what we want to believe. It may seem odd that in order to grow, we need to accept our limits. But mature love can solve problems *within* such limits.

But what if one person grows and the other does not—can the relationship make it? My answer is yes and no. The relationships that fail are those in which one person is unwilling to accept the other's limitations, whether real or imagined. Pushing, pulling, and power struggles override joy and love. On the other hand, successful relationships are those in which people accept their limits and those of others. I recall a couple who in therapy initially stressed changing each other. They later learned to savor each other's uniqueness and to get some of their needs met in other relationships. She became more interested in self-help classes and metaphysics. He continued to get his needs met in the business world and work. Their times together became times of sharing both their differences and their similarities.

Learning Not to Seek Unconditional Love

The key word here is *seek*. In mature love relationships, we no longer "crave" unconditional love from our partners. The only time we needed that kind of care was in the first eighteen months of our lives. We no longer need it from others because *we are* unconditional love. Unconditional love is a state of being that comes from within us— not the other way around. The paradox is that when we stop searching for unconditional love, we are often surprised to find someone loving us just that way. Perhaps it is because when we experience ourselves as unconditional love, we give the safety that invites others to share their love.

Accepting and Respecting Commitment

If I do my thing, and you do your thing
And we don't live up to each other's expectations
We might live, but the world will not survive.
You are you, and I am I together, not by chance
Joining hands, we will find each other beautiful
If not, we can't be helped.

CLAUDE STEINER[5]

In addictive love, commitment often is experienced as a "loss of self." In mature love, the opposite is true; self-esteem is enhanced. We experience commitment as expanding ourselves. We go beyond narcissistic self-gratification to share with, give to, and sacrifice for our beloved ones. Commitment accepts, without resistance, the importance and value of the other person in one's life. This is unlike addictive love, which uses commitment as an excuse for hurtful behaviors, e.g., "I have a right to sex—you are my wife." There is a genuine concern for and commitment to the well-being of the other person. We consider how our actions will affect our relationships. We recognize that autonomy is not always doing "what I want when I want it," but rather taking responsibility for our lives in ways least hurtful to ourselves and others. Autonomy includes boundaries and limits, and mature lovers mutually define the boundaries of their relationship to enhance their commitment. Our commitment expresses our deepest values and transcends our fears.

At the base of many relationship problems is a person's having suffered a betrayal in earlier commitments. Such betrayals can be healed with a new experience of commitment. The commitment is not made to a person, nor focused on outcomes, and it makes no guarantees. Rather, it says, "I am committed to the process of being with you and becoming the best me I can be. I will do my part to maintain the connection even as the form of our relationship changes." Because of the tremendous amount of change we are currently exposed to, committing to the process allows us and our relationships to change and grow as post-modern life demands. Love is not an institution. It is a living process that exhibits the characteristics of life: vitality, change, animation, vigor, movement, evolution, energy, and inherent power. As we commit to the changing process of love, we are more likely to be there for another.[6]

Having High Self-Esteem

How much do you love yourself? In a mature love relationship, both individuals have high senses of self-esteem and well-being. They love themselves without needing to prove it to others. In addictive relationships, our self-esteem often will depend on the response of our partners. In healthy relationships, we trust in ourselves, and our self-esteem is not shaken by disapproval or discord.

I recall a relationship in which I was asked to put the other person on a pedestal. He said, "I need you to look up to me to feel good about myself." My response to my friend was direct: "Putting you up on a pedestal would be a lie. We are equals. I will not do so. While we can affirm each other's worth and goodness, we cannot give each other the self-esteem we lack." The relationship ended, and he continued his search for a partner willing to revere him.

Others may put you on a pedestal, and you may be tempted to stay there and enjoy the view. This is a very dangerous place, for what goes up eventually comes down! Mature love is not a place for inflated egos. I once heard humility defined as a gentle acceptance of oneself. Mature lovers seem to express this quiet self-confidence alone and with each other.

Trusting Our Memory of Our Beloved Ones; Enjoying Solitude

An important indication of true love is our ability to trust our memory of our absent lover so we can accept and enjoy our time alone.

Although we may want to be with our absent lover, we are confident he or she eventually will return. In the meantime, memories of good feelings are enough to satisfy us. Mature love assumes that the individuals involved experienced sufficient response to childhood needs, and that they find it easy to know what they need and to reach out for it. Such lucky people accept their right to be loved; they are open, trusting, and undemanding.

As one lover said to another, "How I feel about you in our separate times is so different from what I've known before. I want to be with you, I think about you, and I feel your presence. I trust our spiritual bond. Anxiety and longing are gone, and I eagerly look forward to our time together. Perhaps it is because you trust our absence, too."

I do not wish to sound naïve. Because of the many betrayals of trust we have likely experienced in love relationships, most of us work very hard to heal and open ourselves to trust once again. This is perhaps the greatest challenge love offers.

Expressing Feelings Spontaneously

In addictive love relationships, partners continually replay familiar dramatic scenes that lead to favorite bad feelings such as confusion, anger, guilt, or shame. Such feelings are referred to as "racket" feelings in that they substitute for feelings that were not acceptable for us to express in our families. If a child was shamed for showing anger, she or he might opt for sadness or excitement instead. We cannot not feel; feelings are electrical chemical responses in the body and must be expressed in some form. In a healthy relationship, lovers spontaneously express feelings based on what is actually happening. These are "reactive" feelings. They make sense to a given situation and motivate a person to action.[7] I feel fear if a tiger comes into the room, and I will freeze or flee. I feel anger when I witness someone acting abusively toward a child, and I assert myself. I feel sad when a person close to me dies, and I grieve my loss. I feel glad when my children succeed at their endeavors, and I celebrate with them. Feelings are expressed, rather than suppressed, when they arise, because feelings expressed won't explode later at inappropriate times. Stored-up frustration and anger will come out sometime—you can be sure of it.

One couple, married for the second time, included in their marriage contract a promise to openly discuss any sign of trouble. Such signs would first appear in the form of uncomfortable feelings. Both knew from earlier experiences that not expressing those feelings could escalate into acting-out behavior, resentment, or closing down. While we may tend to repeat dramatic scenes from the past, healthy love knows we can create different—and better—endings. Our feelings can be just the indicators we need to identify and resolve our differences, and expressing them caringly is important to our well-being.

Welcoming Closeness; Risking Vulnerability

With healthy love, we feel connected to life and all of humankind. We know who we can or cannot trust, and we feel safe exploring. With mature love, we can handle disappointment and pain. In a healthy love relationship, we let go of underlying beliefs and decisions that kept us closed and defensive. We are willing to live a full life alone. We know that belonging comes in many different forms and can exist in ways other than a primary relationship.

As one client said, "Now that I know I can survive pain and loss and I know the joys of openness, I choose to live openly and take risks with others. If my openness is too much by another's standards, so be it—I will let go and know there are many others who desire to share my openness. I cannot be other than who I am. We all have the right to prefer one person over another and to economize our time spent with others. It's okay for someone to not want to be with me and choose another. I have many others I can be intimate with!"

Caring with Detachment

Maturity brings the knowledge that we can care, listen, and respond to other's feelings, but we cannot "fix" or remove all ill feelings in others. Therefore, a sense of caring detachment is a healthy sign in a relationship. The partners say, "I care what you feel and I'm here for you," but not, "Let me feel your pain for you."

When Lea and John first sought counseling, Lea was terribly depressed and John, her husband, felt guilty about that. "I can't seem to spring her from this depression, and I've done everything I can think of," he said. "How am I supposed to feel good when she's so damn blue?" Secretly, he felt like a failure as a man and husband. He believed men were to be heroes, saviors of sad heroines.

They both had to learn that Lea was responsible for her own depression. While John could be understanding and sympathetic, he couldn't conquer it for her. In fact, John would find Lea's state of mind less depressing if he felt less responsible for it. John was relieved when he realized this. Meanwhile, Lea was able to feel less guilty when John quit blaming himself for her depression, and thus she was more readily able to explore its underlying causes. John, less anxious, now offered more support. By letting go, they gave their relationship a chance to grow in strength and character.

Affirming Equality and Personal Power of Ourselves and Others

In true love, lovers recognize each other as equals; they are not caught up in psychological games and one-upmanship. Healthy competition allows each to grow without attempting to exert power over the other. And, confrontation stops pain; it does not inflict it. When two people are content and free as individuals, they are much more likely to have a content and free love relationship.

Power Sharing

In healthy love, power is shared. No longer lost in denial, we acknowledge the draw of power plays, and consciously work toward power sharing. Projecting our shortcomings onto others is replaced with permission to be authentic and passionate about life. Personalizing others' behaviors is replaced with clear boundaries that offer protection and frame our individuality. We then listen to others without taking on their blame-shifting maneuvers or attempting to put them down or out. We stand clearly in our own design, our creativity yearning to be conspicuous. It is no longer a matter of burying our talent but of putting it on display in ways that empower and heal ourselves and our relationships.

Power is viewed, then, not as a measurable commodity, but as an unending source of life energy. It is our personal vitality, vigor, passion, and intensity that command a life-changing presence. It is a statement, "I am here with you as an emotional and spiritual equal. I am your mirror and you are mine."

Unlike power plays that leave us with an ugly feeling, power sharing "enlightens" us. We feel lighter. We are more lighthearted! We are easier to be around. Relationships are nourished. Love merges with power as we penetrate the illusion of separateness and seek healing.

The transition from childish omnipotence to power sharing seems an endless struggle. Yet, with practice, sharing in ways that empower us and affirm the power of others will become more natural.

Below is a list of power-sharing behaviors that support healthy love:

- Being free to state beliefs, values, and thoughts, and to be heard and respected
- Being free to express needs, wants, and feelings, and to ask for support and love
- Being free from ego-driven expectations and outcomes
- Participating cooperatively to empower people in a positive way
- Celebrating another's intelligence, knowledge, and other gifts; letting go of jealousy for what another has
- Being willing to come out from our deepest selves and interact intimately with others, to give and receive
- Expressing personal power in a steady and reliable way—being trustworthy and following through on promises
- Giving of oneself in an emotionally supportive way without overnurturing—just being there is enough

- Compromising—agreeing that we are emotional equals and each can share taking the lead
- Mutual problem solving and decision making—examining together how to do things more effectively
- Owning and sharing mistakes guilt-free; making amends to ourselves and others
- Giving direct, clear answers to questions and requests
- Taking actions that support equality and win-win positions— no one-up or one-down situations
- Accepting others where they are—respecting another person's being while we confront improper behaviors
- Treating others with respect and sensitivity, especially when they are vulnerable
- Having a solid sense of identity and acknowledging the need to share ourselves with others
- Listening, discussing, suggesting, and inviting, rather than telling, bribing, or threatening
- Expressing anger and disappointment without the expectation of change—letting go
- Stopping verbal, emotional, and physical abuse in potent and respectful ways
- Being assertive and not passive or aggressive
- Sharing in making decisions and living with the outcomes
- Being willing to yield or wait, and accepting that we will not always get what we want
- Stating positions clearly, and then respectfully letting go while trusting that the outcome will be positive[8]

In conclusion, mature lovers welcome the needs to love and risk vulnerability. They have faced their aloneness and know the joys of sharing. They know they no longer need people to survive as they once did in childhood, that life is harsh at times, unfair at times, and yet continues to be good.

As I write or talk about healthy love, I notice I have fewer words than when I write or talk about addictive love. And rightly so. Real love is a state of being. It is pure, it is simple, it emanates from within me—a place I cannot clearly define, though it feels like the heart talking to each cell of my being. It is my own creation, going outward. Sometimes I stop it; sometimes I share it.

You have known the experience of love. Each time you reexperience it, tell yourself, "This is love, this is real, and I am experiencing it over and over again."

I Am! And You Are! And Love;
Is All: That Matters!

RICHARD BACH, The Bridge Across Forever[9]

III

*~ *~ *~ *~

Hope for Tomorrow

From Addiction to Love

The highest expression of civilization is not its art but the supreme tenderness that people are strong enough to feel and show toward one another.

NORMAN COUSINS, Human Options[1]

"What is REAL?*" asked the Rabbit one day, when they were lying side by side near the nursery fender, before Nana came to tidy the room. "Does it mean having things that buzz inside you and a stick-out handle?"*

"Real isn't how you are made," said the Skin Horse. "It's a thing that happens to you. When a child loves you for a long, long time, not just to play with, but REALLY *loves you, then you become Real."*

"Does it hurt?" asked the Rabbit.

"Sometimes," said the Skin Horse, for he was always truthful. "When you are Real you don't mind being hurt."

"Does it happen all at once, like being wound up," he asked, "or bit by bit?"

"It doesn't happen all at once," said the Skin Horse. "You become. It takes a long time. That's why it doesn't often happen to people who break easily, or have sharp edges, or who have to be carefully kept. Generally, by the time you are Real, most of your hair has been loved off, and your eyes drop out and you get

*loose in the joints and very shabby. But these things
don't matter at all, because once you are Real you
can't be ugly, except to people who don't understand."*

*"I suppose you are Real?" said the Rabbit. And
then he wished he had not said it, for he thought the
Skin Horse might be sensitive. But the Skin Horse
only smiled.*

*"The Boy's Uncle made me Real," he said. "That
was a great many years ago; but once you are Real
you can't become unreal again. It lasts for always."*

MARGERY WILLIAMS, The Velveteen Rabbit[2]

Viktor Frankl developed a school of existential psychiatry after suffering harrowing experiences as a prisoner in Auschwitz during World War II. He has written of a revelation he had during his darkest days in the concentration camp: "I saw the truth as it is set into song by so many poets, proclaimed as the final wisdom by so many thinkers. The truth that love is the ultimate and highest goal to which man can aspire. The salvation of man is through love and in love. I understand how a man who has nothing left in this world still may know bliss . . . in the contemplation of his beloved. . . . Love goes very far beyond the physical person of the beloved. It finds its deepest meaning in his spiritual being, his inner self."[3]

Addiction to the presence of another is not love; nor is true love anything like addiction. Love and addiction are separate entities that can resemble and be mistaken for each other. Our challenge is to move from addictive love to healthy belonging, for there we experience most profoundly the meaningful inner self Frankl described.

The Way Out

What can you do if you discover you are in an addictive relationship?

First, remember that most relationships have addictive elements. None of us had all of our needs met in childhood. Our parents, being human, failed us at times. Their failures become our weaknesses when we blame them or demand from others what we failed to get. Second, keep in mind that on some level addictive love is perceived as crucial to survival—thus, it won't easily be given up. Third, remember the psychological reasons for your addiction are as unique to you as your fingerprints. Only you can discover what purpose they serve; only you can find what fears keep you from letting go. If you are unable to let go of an unhealthy relationship, or if you find yourself moving from one addictive relationship to another, it's time to seek outside help.

Fourth, work toward intimacy with yourself. When we know that we are complete by ourselves, we are ready for healthy love relationships. Self-sufficiency and self-knowledge can be the keys to love and freedom.

Fifth, remember that moving from addiction to love is a process. Just as there was a way into dependent behavior, there is a way out. There is hope. In knowing the difference between addictive love and healthy belonging, in understanding that process, you can learn acceptance of yourself and others; thus, your chances of achieving fulfillment in love increase.

Out of Addiction and into Healthy Love: The Process

I experienced the ending of a marriage in 1980. To that date, the relationship had been the most significant one in my life, and ending it was very painful. I never thought it could or would happen to me. In my personal journey afterward and in my journey through therapy with others, a clear process with definable stages in and out of such relationships emerged. We went through consistent stages, and as I began clarifying those phases, change became less painful and more acceptable—even welcome. It became much easier to know if a person was staying in a love relationship for right or wrong reasons, or leaving a love relationship for right or wrong reasons. Knowing the difference became critical to knowing what to do and when to do it. There was a sense of relief in knowing the process and in preparing for a positive outcome. Trusting the process became necessary to successfully completing the process. Whether one was currently in or out of a relationship did not matter. One could be involved in the process.

My therapy with couples changed. Getting out of addiction and into healthy love was an "inside job." Attempting to change a relationship without altering the individuals' internal beliefs proved futile. Initial therapy sessions had been settings for power struggles, and I was required to be the judge and referee. This never worked and I ended up feeling drained—a victim.

I had learned from my own unhealthy dependency that I had drawn certain people into my life and had behaved in predictable ways. I had needed to examine my fear of separateness, my fear of having needs, my fear of closeness. I learned I was only responsible for changing myself. I had brought people and situations into my life that fit who I had been at the time. Although I had found others' behavior unacceptable at times, I had to wonder what part of me needed this pain, and why. As I changed, I began inviting healthier people and relationships into my life.

I began working with couples in a more effective way. I saw that who they each were in the relationship made perfect sense. I diffused their power plays by asking them each to journey alone awhile, to discover who they were and how the discord in their relationship made sense to them psychologically. Some were angered by this suggestion and insisted it was the relationship that was in trouble or some other problem. Those who risked the inner journey and stayed with the process learned the key to love is inner freedom.

In the model I have described there are seven stages in moving from addiction to love.

1. Denial
2. Discomfort
3. Confrontation
4. Psychological separation
5. Resolution of self
6. Belonging
7. Reaching out

Denial

In this stage, the relationship often seems to be normal. Perhaps we endured considerable emotional, spiritual, or physical abuse or neglect from a partner, and later denied or rationalized it. We could have a tendency toward dependency on someone who might harm us. In the new relationship, the euphoria of infatuation masks danger signals, but the relationship follows a definite pattern. Giving is often motivated by what others expect or is experienced as losing; fear of true intimacy is dealt with melodramatically, ensuring a level of excitement that substitutes for authentic closeness. Many—perhaps all—of addictive love's characteristics are present, but they are ignored or denied. *Suppression* is a hallmark of this stage.

Here are some beliefs, expressed in common maxims, that support this stage:

"All couples go through this."
"It's better to be in a bad relationship than none at all."
"I took him or her for better or worse."
"That's life."
"Always see the good in people."
"I don't have it so bad."

Addictive lovers fear the truth about themselves. Sometimes only a lack of information keeps a couple in this stage. However, with the right information, one or both partners will begin to move out of the dependent relationship.

Sadly, many couples stay locked in this stage believing this is all there is or the best they can get. Or, if not entrenched in this stage, many couples return to denial when they are faced with the challenges the process of healthy love requires.

Discomfort

In this stage, one or both partners become aware that something is missing. Inner voices say:

"This is not enough."
"Something is not quite right."
"What's wrong with me? I should be happier."
"I wonder if he or she still loves me? I wonder if I still love
    him or her?"
"Is this all there is? I feel bored."
"I feel oppressed; I've got to get out."

In the first stage, we suppressed problems and tried to adapt to the relationship; but in the second stage, *agitation* makes such denial impossible. Such agitation is caused by blocked energy that needs to be expressed in the intimacy and creativity denied in addictive love. At this point, it's a challenge to identify the problem and to resolve it.

Because in this stage our relationships remain primarily addictive, most people begin looking outside themselves and their relationships for solutions or comfort; they may turn to alcohol, food, affairs, work, exercise, religion, gambling, or other processes that hold the potential of becoming obsessions. Although such obsessions may provide initial relief, they don't satisfy a person's longing because they become yet another misguided, addictive attempt to develop self-esteem, find meaning in life, or cover the pain we feel but have not yet clarified.

A person may become aware of recurring emotions, behaviors, and frequent unhappy feelings. Generally, one person, feeling fearful and guilty, begins to move out of the addictive relationship. At this stage, the problem has not been defined, so frustration, confusion, depression, and anxiety are common. Often, one or both partners return to the first stage in resignation to relieve themselves of fear and guilt.

Confrontation

Our desire to grow is accepted. Life may have knocked on our door with an event that shakes us up and wakes us up, so we are now willing to see the disease of our unhealthy dependency. That major life event may be a depression, a separation, a book, treatment for an addiction, a brush with death, an illness, a major life change, a caring confrontation by a friend, the wisdom of experience. Suddenly, problems in the relationship are confronted by one or both individuals. However, in keeping with the relationship's addictive quality, the emphasis tends to be on changing each other to rebalance the relationship. Because one person is threatening to leave, the alarming symptoms escalate. There is more melodrama; accusations, denials, and anger, all of which mask fear, prevail. Both partners try to control the situation. Such attempts to control may take the form of threats, physical abuse, or overadapting in an effort to placate the other. There may be much literal and figurative pushing and pulling.

At this point, a couple may return to a previous stage, decide to separate or divorce, or seek counseling. If they enter therapy, the partners often want the therapist to change the other partner or address symptoms of trouble in the relationship, such as sexual problems or lack of communication. Mundane psychological how-tos—how to have sex, how to communicate, how to fight—do not work! They miss the point: there is much more going on psychologically that both people need to wake up to than just the problems in the relationship.

Secretly, the individuals may fear they failed or did something wrong; they may suffer from guilt or despair. Suppressing these unpleasant feelings, they often place blame elsewhere and become angry. This stage, then, is *characterized by crisis*. It involves much interaction—in fact, too much interaction—that is so negative it compounds the problem. This is the stage where domestic abuse is likely to occur. Homicide, suicide, violence, illness, and other escalations are parts of this stage.

It is unfortunate when separation or divorce occur here. Without self-understanding, people may re-create similar relationships, or limit their feelings of love. Some carry the anger and pain with them for years. To truly heal, we must move on.

Psychological Separation

If the partners possess enough insight and are committed enough to their relationship, one or both of them move into this stage. To be sure, this stage is crucial, time consuming, and often resisted.

Psychological separation is necessary if people are to move from obsessive dependency into healthy, mature relationships. In this stage we become willing to let go of the expectation that a relationship must fulfill our private fears and needs. We are now willing to begin an inward journey of self-discovery, to confront private myths, illusions, and self-promises that contribute to love addiction. Through self-discovery or with the help of therapy, we learn to ask and answer questions such as:

"Who am I?"
"How did I get where I am today?"
"What private promises did I make to myself when I was
     younger?"
"What am I afraid of?"
"Why do I fear separation?"
"Why do I fear closeness?"
"What false attempts have I made to alleviate my fears?"
"What do I believe about women? men? love? power?"

Because psychological separation involves a need to be emotionally detached for a time, the individuals may appear to be egocentric, and they often are unable to feel or express love for the other during this difficult time. *But this is temporary.* Experiencing self-intimacy is important during this period. *Distance,* or *detachment,* is the hallmark of this stage.

Sometimes a physical separation also takes place, although this is not necessary if the individuals give each other the freedom to journey through this stage without terrible tensions. It is easier to accept distance if one realizes one's partner is doing what he or she must in order to develop a capacity for love. Understanding that being distant is a part of the process allows one to not feel guilty.

Until people have a sense of who they are, like who they are, and have healed their wounds and dealt with their fears, they are not psychologically free to love. In the meantime, it is important that a commitment be made to the relationship until one or both partners have the clear understanding of themselves that will allow them to assess the relationship from a new, healthier viewpoint. If one is single, it is important to experience this stage to ensure healthy love relationships in the future. People need to learn to be friends and parents to themselves—a prerequisite to having good relationships with others.

Healthy support systems—friends, family, or support groups—can help affirm self-exploration and change. Because the partners have backed away from each other psychologically during this time, it is a very difficult period. Stress can make it harder, and outside support is needed. In fact, during this time some people revert to old, familiar ways, because self-exploration can be terrifying. If the partners call on their greatest strengths—compassion, patience, tolerance, acceptance, and caring detachment—they'll make it through.

Resolution of Self

At this stage, individuals have answered the question "Who am I?" Through a long, sometimes difficult process, individuals have gained a sense of self-identity, self-esteem, and the knowledge that "I am enough alone." They know what they need and want, what is important, and what is not. They have uncovered the fears and negating beliefs that contributed to problems in their love relationships, and have healed or changed them. It is important that people allow for the necessary time to *integrate* such large changes into their lives and personalities. I once heard that it takes the body six months to incorporate a change into the nervous system.[4] A compulsive need to get results now must not run interference with the process.

People now develop an appreciation for their talents, interests, creative potential, and pursuits. They find a sense of healthy detachment and an awareness of their capacities for intimacy and love. They are comfortable while alone and feel a sense of inner peace. To others, it may seem as if they have matured and accepted reality. They seem to recognize that life consists of new experiences and lessons that provide many options. Life involves choice, action, and consequences—and that fact is no longer terrifying.

It is not uncommon for resistance to appear with questions to test our sincerity. "Are you sure you want to change?" "How do you know

it will be better?" "What if people do not like you anymore?" Sometimes we resort to old behaviors to answer these questions and feel
like we have relapsed. It usually does not take long to realize that we
cannot go back to the way it was. We are different. A ten-year-old may
act like a two-year-old at times, but does not want to remain at two.

Once an individual has gained this self-reliance, it is time to evaluate his or her relationship from this new perspective and decide
whether it should continue. If a person has already left a relationship
or been deserted, he or she now begins to trust that love is possible in
the future. We may even surprise ourselves with a feeling of gratitude
for the painful lessons learned.

Belonging

If the individuals have made it to this stage, they possess a new freedom and a new ability to love maturely. They discover that being in a
love relationship is not the only way to belong—they can also be part
of families, have friends, and belong to support groups. Belonging
comes from an inner belief that says, "I belong in this life and with
meaning."

If couples therapy continues, it now focuses on "we." For the partners are now ready to experience the essence of each other, and there
can be a high level of intimacy. Though they see themselves as
unique and different from each other, they know that their new
closeness allows for individual differences, that the relationship
complements and coexists with individual freedom. Giving is spontaneous; there is emotional and spiritual bonding. Commitment is
characterized by a desire not only to give to the other, but to serve
the other without expecting something in return. A new realism allows for faults, failures, and disappointments. There is equality, and
power plays diminish. The three entities of every relationship—"I,"
"you," and "we"—can now coexist peacefully.

Reaching Out

In this stage, people move from focusing on themselves and their relationships to a more universal giving and experiencing. Content

with themselves and with others, they now have more creative energy, physical stamina, and spiritual strength to help them give and respond. Since they no longer depend on relationships to provide all of life's meaning, they are free to seek additional meaning in life. Adversity now provides opportunities to be more, to experience more. A mature love relationship serves as a springboard for our energy and our interest in the world. Our primary love relationships are the fueling docks that help launch us into life to do what really matters— share our uniqueness with life. But one need not be with a lover to feel energetic or nourished. Love expands from an exclusive relationship to universal love that reinforces the belief that love does, indeed, make the world go 'round. Imagine what the world might look like if we were free to share love and power!

Stages one, two, and three include characteristics of addictive love. To end a relationship here without awareness of that truth is addictive in itself, and we will carry the scars of the relationship with us. Stages four and five reflect independence. They are "I" stages that often seem narcissistic. Here we learn what we were supposed to learn in late adolescence and early adulthood: autonomy, spontaneity, and the capacity for intimacy. Stages six and seven reflect healthy belonging: interdependency alternating with healthy dependency. Going through these stages is not always smooth. We may be in level six one day and in level two the next. As we climb upward, we spend more time in the higher levels. Keep in mind that one person in a relationship can stay in a lower level as another moves through to level seven. We can only be where we are ready to be. Those on a higher level are challenged to be more patient. Couples therapy is a struggle in the first three stages, but quite simple in stage six after people have done their individual work in stages four and five. Then there is a sense of understanding and openness to new ways of being together. To further complicate matters, thinking about this from a holistic viewpoint, we can be in all seven stages at the same time. We have the potential of each stage within us at all times. Thus, the choices we make in our love relationships do make a difference. With knowledge and experience we do become wiser.

From Addiction to Healthy Love

What follows is the story of Carly and Dave, a couple in their thir-
ties who moved successfully from an addictive relationship to a
healthier, more mature relationship. Following their situation was
inspirational and educational for me as a therapist. There were
times when the relationship seemed doomed and therapy seemed to
be of little help. The pain and isolation Carly and Dave felt during
their ordeal were often great, yet they trusted that change was possible, and they were willing to spend the necessary time and energy to
improve their marriage.

ℯ⮞   ℯ⮞   ℯ⮞

Carly and Dave needed to let go and discover who they were as individuals. Only then could they come back together and choose each
other again—not because of need, but because of new love, respect,
and desire for each other. Their relationship is now alive with excitement, caring, and a new ability to resolve conflicts. Observing Dave
and Carly confirmed my belief that many potentially good marriages
end too early because of addictive qualities that mar the relationships. Sometimes, love simply needs to grow up.

Carly's Story

"In a four-year period, my husband and I changed our residence
three times, moving about eight hundred miles each time. Two of the
moves were made to enhance his career. Although I had a choice in
these decisions, I acted out of fear and duty rather than free choice.
After the third move, I was angry about having to put together a
résumé and find a job each time we relocated. And when I had to
coach my husband on how to vie for a job he really wanted, I thought,
Stop, Carly. What do you want from your life? You're living through him.

"As I started looking for a job after our third move, I was angry
and depressed. I had always been a happy person before; I wanted
that contentment back. I got the name of a counselor and began to
find out why I wasn't content. Among the things I found was that I

needed to learn how to be a separate person from my family, my husband, and my friends. I needed to find out who I was. I thought I had already done that.

"I began to learn that I thought Dave's and most other people's feelings and needs came before my own. I also gave others the kind of power I had granted to my parents as a child. I had believed I was responsible for their thoughts and feelings. Because I believed other people knew better, I hardly trusted my own thoughts and feelings, or my ability to make major decisions or to solve problems. Thus, my life fit well with Dave's, who believed his needs came first and that he had to take care of me and do the thinking and decision making for both of us.

"I also discovered that because anger had not been expressed in either of our families, we weren't truly honest with one another when a problem arose.

"I didn't feel I could ever be mistaken; I thought I had to be perfect. If I did bungle something, I thought something was wrong with me. Dave was also very concerned with perfection and was very critical of any mistakes he or I made. Therefore, I avoided making risky decisions and trying out new things because I was afraid of Dave's reactions.

"I relied on Dave to meet most of my needs, yet I didn't know how to ask for things. I expected him to read my mind. Once I did learn to ask, it seemed like he wasn't available for comfort and support. I didn't know how he felt most of the time because he didn't express his feelings. When I'd ask him how he felt, he often said he didn't know. I also learned through counseling that I often did the feeling for both of us, and let my feelings control me.

"When I shared my discoveries about myself with Dave, he listened, but he didn't understand or accept all of them. I was learning to feel and express anger, and I was learning to act appropriately on my feelings and not always suppress them. It was scary to feel anger toward Dave. At first, I would angrily overreact to small irritations because anger seemed strange; no one had taught me to handle it when I was a child.

"At this time, I was feeling more and more oppressed in my

marriage. If I were single, I thought, I could spend more time with my friends, with people I liked whom Dave didn't like. I also sensed that I wanted more in my marriage. I guess I didn't realize that what I wanted was more intimacy; I just knew something was missing.

"I became pregnant, although it was definitely unplanned. My husband did not want children, but even knowing that and that the timing wasn't the best, I was strongly against getting an abortion. Dave and I decided to continue with the pregnancy, although he said, 'I don't know if I want to share you after all the time we've spent together and things we've done, just the two of us.'

"Just after we decided to continue with the pregnancy, Dave went on a business trip. When he returned, he told me he had been attracted to a single woman he had met on the trip and that he, too, had been feeling restless and unsatisfied in the marriage. He felt that he wanted to be married to me, but he wasn't sure how he felt about this other woman—maybe he wanted to be with her. This was the first time he had been seriously attracted to another woman since he and I started dating fifteen years before. He kept saying it was only a friendship, yet he didn't know how he felt toward me any longer. He seemed to have a strong need for the friendship with Rita, the other woman, and in my gut, I didn't trust that their relationship was just a friendship.

"Dave agreed to see a marriage counselor with me. At first, I was afraid I was going to be left alone and I cried a lot. The support from my counselor and counseling group was invaluable. I finally became strong enough to ask Dave to end the relationship with Rita. He was reluctant to do so, but about a month after my request, he severed his ties with Rita. He was angry at me, which was a new experience for me. Because I had always attended to his feelings before my own, I felt guilty that I was asking him to end the relationship, yet I knew it was interfering with our marriage and working against changes we were making in our relationship. His affection for Rita also kept us from looking at some aspects of our marriage that needed changing.

"Though I continued to change and grow, I felt a real void in my life. I like myself; I knew I could solve problems and decide things for myself. I could decide whom I wanted to be with; I could cope with whatever problems came my way. I could feel deeply and yet still think for myself—I didn't need Dave to do that for me. Although I could ask for help, support, and love from Dave and others, I didn't need them to make me feel complete.

"Once I became a separate person and knew that physical, emotional, intellectual, and spiritual boundaries separated me and Dave, I could choose to be dependent or independent, strong or weak, and not just fall into a role. I could choose to go somewhere or do something with Dave even though I wasn't as excited about it as he was. This differed from my old stance of automatically going along whether I wanted to or not because Dave's needs came first.

"Eight months passed in which Dave struggled with his feelings about me and the marriage. Meanwhile, I had lost the baby.

"One night we got into a terrible argument and Dave said things that hurt me deeply. Something inside of me changed; I told Dave I could accept that he didn't know how he felt about us, but I would not accept his biting comments. I told him I didn't want to hear them again. I guess I was at the point where I'd decided I was ready to get on with my life, with or without Dave. I was tired of his lack of commitment. He needed to decide if he was in or out of the marriage so we could either really work together on improving what we had or go on with our lives separately. At this point, Dave made his decision. He decided he was committed enough to try to improve our relationship.

"Nevertheless, for the next six months, I felt a great space between us, and Dave didn't feel very close to me. A lot of games we'd played had ended. I started to spend more time with close friends and realized what I had heard in counseling was true—that you can't depend on one person to meet all your needs. I found when I was with friends, I'd laugh and have fun. I also spent time alone during this time, trying to develop my spiritual side.

"I even had more to offer Dave now. We began to share what we were learning about ourselves. It was open, honest communication. Sometimes it was very difficult to bring up something that was painful or uncomfortable, but I was learning we could be close, even through pain and anger. We were told that feeling distant was a normal part of ultimately growing together again, and though it scared us, we stuck with each other through this time. After Dave began to understand why he still didn't feel close to me, I started to notice a change for the better in him.

"The therapist suggested then that we start to look at the 'we.' Although I trusted her, I felt some resistance in my gut to doing so. But we began to study the relationship and to ask how we could improve it and purge it of dependency.

"I learned in looking at the 'we' that there may be times when I really wouldn't choose to spend my time the way Dave would or with the same people he would, but if he'd like me to be with him, I would because it's important to him and because I love him. But now I would do it to enhance our bond, not because I was automatically going along with him.

"Now things were definitely starting to improve between us. It was as I had always heard but never before experienced: when I quit looking for unconditional love, it was there. I felt happy about myself, and my happiness was much less dependent on Dave or anyone else than it had ever been. Dave began to honestly share feelings with me, and I felt he respected my thoughts and feelings more than he ever had. He showed a willingness to really listen. I also was more open to him, knowing now I could say no, and therefore, I was more willing to take suggestions or advice from him. He began to do things for me and to complement me in a most pleasing way.

"Our marriage isn't perfect, and I know achieving intimacy is a long, difficult process. It's exciting now because we can laugh, joke, and have fun with each other, yet we also are free to be angry and we don't always have to 'make everything okay' when it isn't. We also can be separate from each other; if one of us is feeling down, the other can be supportive but not become depressed also. And we know we can have close, separate friends and still be close to each other.

"When I began counseling for myself, I had no idea where it would lead. I just knew I wanted to be happy again. The entire process with myself and with my marriage has been very painful at times. Yet, it has also been exciting and rewarding. I feel I rediscovered parts of myself I had lost touch with. I've also developed new parts of myself to become more of a complete person. I have a real, growing, honest, spontaneous relationship with my husband that feels very good. I love him much more freely than before. It was well worth the risk, work, and time to reach this point. I think I've learned communication skills that will stay with me the rest of my life. And now we're looking forward to the birth of our first child."

Dave's Story

"Looking back now, I can see it was a crisis, although at the time it didn't seem that way. It just seemed as if things kept getting more and more complicated until finally there was no room to move.

"Still, I don't think I would have sought counseling as a solution. It was Carly who suggested we see a therapist together. I never really thought of it as marriage counseling at first. We were just seeing her therapist. I'm sure it was made easier by the fact that Carly already had been attending weekly group therapy sessions.

"For most of the time Carly and I had known each other, our relationship wasn't especially healthy. We didn't know that, of course. We thought everything was fine, operating under the same system that had brought us together back in high school.

"I was the one who had to be strong, be in control, be special, be 'one-up.' When we went to a party, I had to get the laughs. When we were going to go somewhere for the weekend, I was the one who decided where we'd go. I remember at that time a lot of my humor demeaned Carly.

"I also was the peacemaker, as I had been while growing up in my family (or had thought I had to be). Carly and I rarely fought or even had serious arguments because I thought that was bad. I thought we could never disagree. We both swallowed our feelings and 'went along,' and we thought that was just swell.

"I swallowed my feelings a lot. It wasn't okay to feel. Big boys don't cry. I had never had an intimate talk with my mom or my dad. In our family, we laughed things off. If it was negative, we'd bury it. As a result, I couldn't even ask for the simplest things—a back rub, time alone, sexual intimacy.

"But I found someone who took care of all that for me—without my even asking. When we were trying to decide what to do for an evening or weekend, Carly would wait to see what I wanted to do, then go along with it. She offered to rub my back; she got real value out of taking care of me. Of course, I didn't know that. I just knew that for some magical reason, I was getting taken care of. But there was no intimacy or shared feelings.

"Then things started to change. I suppose it began when Carly started therapy. She started changing her part of our system. No more demeaning humor, she said. She quit taking care of me so much. She began to have her own friends, her own life. I was no longer the one in control. The time I remember most vividly was the first time she got really mad at me. I knew things were no longer the same.

"I remember criticizing Carly for being dependent on me; that bugged me. I hated it when she'd try to figure out what I wanted to do, then, once we did it, I'd find out she'd really have rather done something else. Yet, at the same time, I'm sure I was beginning to feel scared that she was no longer dependent on me!

"It was a very mixed-up time for me. It doesn't surprise me now, looking back, that I began to want to pull away from Carly then. Something—I didn't know what—was wrong in our relationship. Yet, at the same time, there was someone new who seemed to be able to give me more of what I needed.

"The crisis that led to our seeing a therapist grew out of a business trip I'd made with a group of people. I became strongly attracted during this week to another member of the group, Rita, a woman about my age. I didn't know how to deal with the feelings I had for this woman. I was strongly attracted to her, but I knew I couldn't act on those feelings. She was also attracted to me, and we decided to keep in touch on a friendship basis following our trip.

"It became clear to me in the days following the trip that my feelings for Rita were more than friendship, and I fantasized about somehow being able to be with her in the future. But at the same time, I didn't want to ruin ten years of marriage.

"For the first time I found myself questioning whether I wanted to spend the rest of my life with Carly. Did I love her? Did I love her for the same reasons I had fallen in love with her fifteen years before?

"I found myself constantly caught in the middle, trying very hard to build a new friendship by long distance with Rita, and at the same time trying to assure Carly that everything was all right. It was one of the most uncomfortable times in my life. What bugged me most was that Carly couldn't understand my desire for the friendship. I thought she was being restrictive and jealous, and we had lots of discussions and arguments about that.

"I remember that we talked about how this whole thing had happened. Carly had been making some noticeable personal changes through therapy, but I couldn't see how that was affecting our relationship. I just figured things were going along as usual. It never occurred to me that the changes in her would change the way I felt about her.

"Well, things just kept getting worse for Carly and me. I was always in the middle, trying harder and harder to make Carly and my new friend understand why the other felt the way she did. As I learned later, this 'middleman' position was a familiar place for me, for I had always tried to make everyone happy.

"I thought about separating from Carly; I even thought about divorce. I didn't find either very acceptable, but nevertheless, they were options. I'm not sure why I didn't exercise either of them. For one thing, I was probably too scared. And somewhere, beneath all this mess, I think I believed we'd gone too far just to give up.

"By this time, I'd begun weekly group therapy sessions. I had almost no emotional connection to Carly. I had said I was committed to the relationship, and I was. I had decided I would give it about the only thing I felt I could—time. And I also had agreed to begin looking at myself and my role in our marriage by going to a counselor.

"At first, I merely used counseling sessions to deal with my anger and sadness about not being able to continue my new friendship. But at the same time, I began to find out why I was the person I was, and that was fascinating. I learned so much about myself, and the more I learned, the more clear my current predicament seemed. I could begin to figure out how things had gotten to where they were, what some of my lifelong beliefs and behavior patterns were, and where they had come from.

"Still, times weren't easy. I still wanted to pull away from Carly, even more so when I started discovering something about myself and having more of a sense of myself. All my life with Carly, it had been 'us.' Now there was a 'me' again that I liked. That part of me wanted to go off on my own and not slog through all this muck of trying to rebuild a relationship.

"Before therapy, I had focused on Carly and thought about how she should be different, but now I was looking almost entirely at myself. I still didn't feel especially connected to Carly, but I could begin applying some things I had learned about myself to our relationship.

"I think the one way therapy helped most was to confirm my belief that things could be better in time. I was willing, even though I felt far away from Carly on a day-to-day basis, to give us time.

"We aren't talking weeks here. I was in group therapy for more than a year. Carly continued in therapy at the same time, too. Finally, very slowly, I began to feel closer to Carly again. I mean very slowly. There had been so many times when I didn't think I could ever feel close to her again.

"It was intriguing to see us beginning to have a healthier relationship again. It sure wasn't puppy love or romantic infatuation or anything like that. Carly wasn't instantly a new woman, nor was I a new man. But we both knew ourselves a lot better than we ever had before, and we both had learned a lot about how to have a healthy relationship. We knew what had attracted us the first time we fell in love fifteen years earlier. Now the trick was to see if it would work all over again—for a different set of reasons.

"At some point, when Carly and I were both well along in therapy, the therapist said she thought it might be time for us to see her together again. We did, and she said she felt we'd each been working on the 'me' for quite a while, and that it was time to begin looking again at the 'we.'

"As logical as that seemed, I'm not sure it would ever have

occurred to me. I was still into my journey of self-discovery, and now that I had gotten past a lot of pain, it was even more enjoyable. But I think she was right.

"Gradually, our relationship became calmer and happier again. We seemed to be coming back together in a new way. I didn't have to feel in control anymore; I began to let go in many situations where I once would have had to be in charge.

"And we looked at the 'we' again. It has been some time since all this happened. We are feeling good again. The closeness has come back; I think it's safe to say we're in love again—in a much different way than we used to be. And I think we're still in the beginning stages of our new relationship. I think we'll continue to feel more and more emotionally connected.

"The whole process has been amazing to me. It is ironic to think that in order to become a healthy couple again, two people have to travel separate ways for a while. They don't have to be physically separated—and I'm glad we weren't. But they have to be psychologically distant before they can come together again. Until each is willing to step aside and examine his or her role in the relationship, I think it's almost impossible to change. But I feel that making that separate, inner journey and bringing what I learned from it back to our new relationship has been the most meaningful and rewarding experience of my life."

Sometimes, We Need to Let Go

Sometimes, our relationships cannot be salvaged, and we must be willing to say good-bye to them, even though we feel compelled to stay. "Every happy plot ends in a marriage knot" says the old song, but the assumption that love relationships are always meant to be lifelong is simply erroneous. When we feel vulnerable to the thought of life outside a particular relationship, we often hang in there and attempt to control it instead. In such situations, we must discern whether we are there to satisfy addictive compulsions or a passion that emanates from our deeper truth—the heart, soul, body

connection discussed in chapter 6. While passion can be an important part of healthy love, the compelling high must not pull us off
course. The pull of sexual or romantic attraction can be so strong
that we begin denying the obvious—that the relationship cannot
work except as mutual addiction. Attraction can come with light-
ning speed, trumpets and cymbals that defy all words and suggest a
mystical connection. Sometimes it is. On the other hand, it can also
be a magnetic pull to self-destruction.

ᕽ   ᕽ   ᕽ

Dan's story is of a type I have witnessed many times. Yet, I also know
that we do not see what we need to see, let go of people we need to let
go of, until we are ready to see and let go. Sometimes, as in Dan's
case, one needs to get "sick and tired" before one is willing to move
on in one's process.

At first, Dan was reluctant to seek help for his addictive relationship because he was a successful counselor and felt he should know
all the answers. He saw himself as a strong, independent, handsome
man with high self-esteem, and it was hard for him to admit he felt
otherwise. He had relied on himself for a long time. But Dan learned
that real strength came through his inward odyssey and discovery of
things that kept him in an unhealthy relationship.

When Dan first sought help, his life seemed out of control. He
was physically abusive when angry, he drank too much, and he suffered from high blood pressure and migraine headaches. It was clear
that if he didn't change, he would continue on a self-destructive
course. He came into therapy to regain control of his life.

Unlike Carly and Dave, Dan needed to leave his relationship in
order to move ahead with his life, something he initially could not
imagine doing. His theme, like the themes of so many others trapped
in love addiction, was "I can't imagine living without her."

"To begin, I think I must go back to my childhood and my relationship with my father. I don't think I ever felt loved by my father.
Although I now believe my father did, in fact, love me, I don't think
he found the words very easy to say or the feelings very easy to display. I don't recall my father ever telling me he loved me.

"As I matured, I think I failed to realize some of these things about my father, and I thought I was not a very lovable person, although I presented myself as confident and capable. As I later reflected on my relationship with my father, I realized the only time I ever felt my father loved me was when I worked extremely hard on our family-owned farm, when my father did or said things to show he was pleased. I subsequently carried this striving for love over into my adult relationships. I believed I needed another's love to affirm my right to live. I also think this need to be loved led me to marry at the very young age of nineteen. This marriage was a mistake from the start, but I stayed in it for twelve years. I did so mainly because of insecurity; I felt I was not a lovable person.

"When the marriage—in which I was extremely unhappy for years—became absolutely intolerable, I filed for a divorce. Shortly after the divorce, I met Ann, also recently divorced. In a short time, we became friends and lovers. But this relationship was extremely addictive.

"Both Ann and I had feelings of not being able to live without the other. Shortly after starting to date, we moved in together. Very early in the relationship, it seemed Ann and I allowed the relationship to consume and control us. We spent little time outside the relationship, and maintained few outside interests. We feared losing each other. We were completely obsessed with our relationship, each of us expecting the other to meet all our needs, never realizing just how impossible such a thing was.

"Shortly, problems sprang up. The relationship became extremely painful for me when Ann started to see other men, reinforcing my belief that I was not very lovable. Although this caused me great pain and anxiety, I stayed because I was addicted to the relationship and did not know how to get out 'without dying,' as I would have said then. I feel the most addictive aspect of our relationship was that we demanded unconditional love from each other no matter what our behavior was and no matter how much we did to destroy the relationship.

"I think that at this time I kept telling myself I could change Ann if I loved her enough. I *had* to change her because I could not live without her! I was not a whole person without my relationship with her. This very addictive relationship became more and more destructive for me, and I think for Ann, too. The destructiveness of our bond began to affect me; my drinking increased and my behavior became more and more self-destructive.

"Finally, because of my behavior, someone whom I greatly respected asked me to take a serious look at where I was heading and to try to bring my life under control. At this time, I realized my explosive anger, my bad feelings about myself, and my unhealthy relationship with Ann were things I was unable to deal with by myself.

"So I sought help from a therapist. I feel this is where I realized many things about my life, and I soon realized I had to end my unhappy, unhealthy relationship. I finally was able to do so after a number of therapy sessions. I truly believe that had it not been for my entering therapy, this addictive relationship would have subsequently destroyed me, if not both of us.

"I learned that unconsciously, I had sought out a woman who could not love me intimately, supporting my belief that I was unlovable or a disappointment to others. As I began to be good to myself, changing my beliefs about my worth and accepting that my parents had loved me the best they could, I began to choose women who were capable of love and intimacy. I learned I was the one who feared the hurt and pain of rejection, and who had believed it wasn't safe to be close. So I had chosen Ann to avoid getting truly close. It was great to discover I actually had a choice!

"Since that time, I have made some big changes in my life, such as moving to a new area. Admittedly, this was one of the hardest decisions I've ever made. Since my relationship with Ann ended, I've had occasion to see her. While I certainly like Ann, I don't feel we could ever have a good, healthy relationship. Because of this, I have no desire to become involved with her again. Since escaping from that addictive relationship, I've become more comfortable with being alone. I feel I have grown a lot, and I hope to continue for the rest of my life. I look forward to loving and feeling close to a woman. Now I believe real love is possible, and that I deserve it!"

❧   ❧   ❧

Carly, Dave, and Dan have come a long way. If you see a bit of yourself in their situations, read on: you, too, can learn how to put love and freedom simultaneously to work in your life.

> *If you bring forth what is within you, what you bring forth will save you. If you do not bring forth what is within you, what you do not bring forth will destroy you.*

> The Gospel According to Thomas[5]

Helping Yourself out of Love Addiction

The highest goal a therapist can have for clients is to instill in them the knowledge that solutions to their problems lie within, then to pass on tools to help guide people to those powerful inner answers. This chapter attempts to provide you with skills that will allow you to act as your own therapist and to address your relationship problems in a helpful, hopeful way.

We've discussed the roots of love addiction, described its characteristics, and studied the process of moving from troublesome dependency to mature, fulfilling love. As we've seen, the roots of love addiction run deep, and the road out is often long and rough. So long and rough, in fact, that you may be asking yourself: Why bother? Isn't any love better than no love at all?

Why expel love addiction from your life? There is an extremely good answer to that challenge: *because addictive love is limiting.*

It limits your ability to feel content
It limits your ability to function and to live up to your potential
It limits your openness to new experiences
It limits your ability to enjoy and live in the present
It limits your energy for creative pursuits
It limits your personal power and your freedom
It limits your ability to accept others
It limits your willingness to face your fears
It limits your spontaneity

It limits your level of consciousness and your spiritual potential
It limits your capacity for intimacy and your ability to truly love

You must decide for yourself what choices you'll make for your
life. You surely do not have to change, but if you do decide to change,
make sure you're doing it for yourself. Once you decide to forgo addictive love, once you stop seeing life in melodramatic black and
white and start seeing it in true, complex color, it may be difficult or
impossible for you to retreat to your old way of thinking. You'll find
you can invite—but not pull or coerce—others in your life to come
along with you. If they resist, you'll do well to be patient and compassionate. You may even find that your decision to give up addictive
love means you'll have to end your troublesome relationship completely, a decision that surely will cause you some very natural grief.

Fulfillment never comes easily; there are no guarantees that your
choice to change will bring you instant happiness. As this book's descriptive sketches have illustrated, some who risked change grew into
healthier love relationships, while others found they had to let go of
their relationships and get new starts in life and love.

Once you decide to free yourself from love addiction, you agree to
let go of your desire to be controlled or to control another; you cease
to manipulate others to get what you need and want. The urge to
manipulate others is a powerful one, and in giving it up you'll no
doubt experience some grief. But in the long run, such suffering will
be far less than the pain you may have inflicted on yourself or another via an addictive relationship.

This chapter is dedicated to those who opt for healthier, happier
love. Those of you who feel uncertain about how you wish to pro-
ceed may want to experiment with the exercises that follow; see what
you can learn about yourself. Those of you who wish, for whatever
reasons of your own, to maintain the status quo in your troublesome
relationship may want to stop here. You're being honest, but remember, the decision against change is yours—so give up blaming others
for your relationship troubles. You must remember that you've relin-
quished personal power and growth to love addiction.

Some of you may doubt the statement that most, if not all, love
relationships harbor some elements of addiction. To you, I suggest

doing the following exercises before you decide it can't be true. The exercises are based on the premises that much of who we are is not in our conscious awareness most of the time, and that awareness precedes change.

Change = awareness + action. These exercises are designed to help increase awareness and motivate action.

I have designed the exercises based on my experience as a psychotherapist and workshop leader; some are combined with my personal knowledge. I have found that the exercises are helpful for people who wish to purge their lives of addictive behavior. Although all therapy is basically self-therapy, these exercises are usually done with professional guidance. In the event you find it difficult to use them on your own, or if moving through them elicits information or feelings that make you uncomfortable, don't hesitate to seek professional support.[1]

Some of the exercises may require a great amount of thought and time. They are not designed to be completed hurriedly, which will be obvious as you move through them. The time and thought you put into them will probably grow into a self-help process that spans several months. Some exercises will mean more to you than others do. Though their purpose is serious, they are designed to be fun.

Good luck on your personal journey toward self-discovery. My hope is that you will discover at least one personal insight that alters your life for the better; my wish for you is more joy, freedom, wisdom, and love.

The Self-Help Method

Listed here are seven basic steps that will help you move from love addiction to healthy love:

1. *Awareness:* admitting that love addiction plays a role in your life
2. *Assessment:* discovering the extent of your love addiction
3. *Decision:* using your personal power to move out of addiction
4. *Exploration:* examining your personal fears, myths, and history

5. *Reprogramming:* letting go of the old; embracing the new
6. *Renewal:* moving toward mature love
7. *Expansion:* developing personal uniqueness and the ability to truly love yourself and others

Awareness Exercises:
Admitting That Love Addiction Plays a Role in Your Life

The fact that you chose this book, and perhaps others similar to it, indicates you already know your love relationship has addictive aspects. Without such an admission, you might still be trapped in the denial stage, where there is no fertile ground for the seeds of change to grow. The information in this book is designed to help you move from awareness that a problem exists into the next important steps: recognizing your dependency problem and gaining control over it.

Exercise 1-A: Recognition

Remember the first time you heard the term "love addiction." Now, read the questions that follow, then close your eyes and visualize your responses.

What did you think and feel when you first heard the term?
What made you decide to read a book about love addiction?
Were there feelings of hesitation about reading it?
What fears, if any, were a part of such resistance?
How do you hope to be different after reading this book?

Assessment Exercises:
Discovering the Extent of Your Love Addiction

The following exercises can help you evaluate the either addictive or healthy qualities in your relationships. It is assumed that the fewer addictive characteristics your relationship has, the higher its quality.

Exercise 2-A: How Does Your Relationship Rate?

With your current love relationship in mind, carefully read first the characteristics of addictive love, then those of healthy love. Score

your relationship for each addictive love characteristic based on the
following scale: 0 = never; 1 = rarely; 2 = sometimes; 3 = often;
4 = almost always; 5 = always. Then score yourself for healthy love.

Addictive Love	**Healthy Love**
__ Feels all-consuming	__ Allows for individuality
__ Cannot define ego boundaries	__ Experiences and enjoys both oneness with and separateness from partner
__ Has elements of sadomasochism	__ Brings out best qualities in both partners
__ Fears letting go	__ Accepts endings
__ Fears risk, change, and the unknown	__ Experiences openness to change and exploration
__ Allows little individual growth	__ Invites growth in both partners
__ Lacks true intimacy	__ Experiences true intimacy
__ Plays psychological games	__ Feels freedom to ask honestly for what is wanted
Gives to get something back	__ Experiences giving and receiving in the same way
__ Attempts to change the partner	__ Does not attempt to change or control the partner
__ Needs partner to feel complete	__ Encourages self-sufficiency of partner
__ Seeks solutions outside of self	__ Accepts limitations of self and partner
__ Demands and expects unconditional love	__ Does not insist on unconditional love
__ Refuses commitment (antidependency)	__ Can make commitment
__ Looks only to partner for affirmation and worth	__ Has high self-esteem and sense of well-being
__ Fears abandonment upon routine separation	__ Trusts memory of beloved; enjoys solitude
__ Re-creates familiar negative feelings	__ Expresses feelings spontaneously

Addictive Love	*Healthy Love*
__ Desires, yet fears, closeness	__ Welcomes closeness; risks vulnerability
__ Attempts to "take care" of partner's feelings	__ Cares, but can remain detached
__ Plays power games ("one-upmanship")	__ Affirms equality and personal power of self and partner

Now, add the scores for each list and divide by twenty to get a numerical average for each. Does your relationship exhibit more symptoms of trouble than of health?

Exercise 2-B: You and Your Other Relationships
Think about your relationships to other people, such as friends, co-workers, or relatives. Score your relationships for each characteristic based on the following scale: 0 = never; 1 = rarely; 2 = sometimes; 3 = often; 4 = almost always; 5 = always. If the scores here indicate your relationships in general are often addictive, you may want to direct serious attention toward gaining and sustaining healthier bonds to others.

Addictive Love	*Healthy Love*
__ Feels all-consuming	__ Allows for individuality
__ Cannot define ego boundaries	__ Experiences and enjoys both oneness with and separateness from partner
__ Has elements of sadomasochism	__ Brings out best qualities in both partners
__ Fears letting go	__ Accepts endings
__ Fears risk, change, and the unknown	__ Experiences openness to change and exploration
__ Allows little individual growth	__ Invites growth in both partners
__ Lacks true intimacy	__ Experiences true intimacy
__ Plays psychological games	__ Feels freedom to ask honestly for what is wanted
__ Gives to get something back	__ Experiences giving and receiving in the same way

Addictive Love	*Healthy Love*
__ Attempts to change the partner	__ Does not attempt to change or control the partner
__ Needs partner to feel complete	__ Encourages self-sufficiency of partner
__ Seeks solutions outside of self	__ Accepts limitations of self and partner
__ Demands and expects unconditional love	__ Does not insist on unconditional love
__ Refuses commitment (antidependency)	__ Can make commitment
__ Looks only to partner for affirmation and worth	__ Has high self-esteem and sense of well-being
__ Fears abandonment upon routine separation	__ Trusts memory of beloved; enjoys solitude
__ Re-creates familiar negative feelings	Expresses feelings spontaneously
__ Desires, yet fears, closeness	__ Welcomes closeness; risks vulnerability
__ Attempts to "take care" of partner's feelings	__ Cares, but can remain detached
__ Plays power games ("one-upmanship")	__ Affirms equality and personal power of self and partner

Exercise 2-C: Relationship Connections

Study the following list illustrating the different areas of contact that connect you and your partner. Now, on a 0-to-10 scale, with 10 being the highest, rate your love relationship.

Area of Contact	*Rating*
• *Physical* (degree of attraction, affection; quality of sexual relationship, physical nurturing)	____
• *Emotional* (degree of expression, communication, support between partners, emotional trust)	____

- *Social*
  (mutual compatibility with friends, family;
  quality of social life)   ____
- *Mental*
  (quality of ideas/information exchange; mutual problem
  solving; acceptance of changing ideas and opinions)   ____
- *Behavioral*
  (quality of partners' treatment of each other and
  support for individual differences)   ____
- *Spiritual*
  (mutual values and attitudes; support for individual
  development)   ____

If there are one or more zeros, the relationship probably is addictive; if your scores are fours or less, the relationship probably needs attention.

Exercise 2-D: How Do I Love Me?

Your self-image plays a significant role in your relationships—the higher your self-esteem, the better your relationships are likely to be. By going through the process of answering these questions, you will become more aware of your own level of self-esteem.

1. How much do you like yourself?
2. As a child, how much did you think or feel your mother liked you?
3. As a child, how much did you think or feel your father liked you?
4. As you grew up, how much did you think or feel your peers liked you?
5. Do you *want* to like yourself better?
6. How much do you look to others for approval?
7. How much do you think or feel your partner likes you?

Exercise 2-E: Power Plays
The following are power plays that often appear in addictive relationships. To the left of each power play, write "yes" or "no" based on whether you have experienced that symptom in your relationship. Note how many "yes's" and "no's" you have.

Since power plays are characteristic of addiction, any "yes" indicates some degree of trouble in the relationship. The more times you wrote "yes," the more attention you'll want to pay to the presence of harmful manipulation in your relationship.

Common Power Plays

_____ Giving advice but not accepting it

_____ Having difficulty in reaching out and asking for support and love

_____ Giving orders; demanding and expecting too much from others

_____ Being judgmental; using put-downs that sabotage the other's success; faultfinding; persecuting; punishing

_____ Holding out on others; not giving what others want or need

_____ Making, then breaking, promises; causing others to trust us and then breaking the trust

_____ Smothering or overnurturing the other

_____ Patronizing, condescending treatment of the other that sets one partner up as superior, the other as inferior; intimidation

_____ Making decisions for the other; discounting the other's ability to solve problems

_____ Putting the other in "no-win" situations

_____ Attempting to change the other (and unwillingness to change the self)

_____ Attacking the other when he or she is most vulnerable

_____ Showing an antidependent attitude ("I don't need you")

_____ Using bullying, bribing behavior; using threats

_____ Showing bitterness, or self-righteous anger; holding grudges

_____ Abusing others verbally or physically

_____ Being aggressive and defining it as assertiveness

_____ Needing to win or be right

____ Resisting stubbornly or being set in one's own way
____ Having difficulty admitting mistakes or saying "I'm sorry"
____ Giving indirect, evasive answers to questions
____ Defending any of the above behaviors

Decision Exercises:
Using Your Personal Power to Move out of Addiction

You've assessed your relationships, and if you found signs of trouble, you now have a decision to make. If you've discovered that your relationships are addictive to some degree—perhaps to a great degree—you now must decide whether to maintain the status quo or to work toward change.

Note: If you are clearing out compulsive habits you may initially feel more compulsive. When letting go of an unhealthy dependency, your feeling of neediness may escalate. These are signs that your process is in motion. Make sure a solid support system is in place. And use it!

Exercise 3-A: What Do You Get from Your Relationships?
We cling to relationships, even troubled ones, because they serve us on some level. Perhaps we gain feelings of self-esteem and security; a sense of belonging; sensations of pleasure, comfort, and success; avoidance of fear; or a sense of meaning in our lives. Think carefully about how your relationships serve or protect you. Taking plenty of time to answer this question, make a list of secondary gains you are receiving from your current relationship. Try to be honest with your answers. We introduce now a set of rituals designed to help you concentrate on your relationship and its qualities. You will be making the following statements based on how you have been in your relationship in the past. Place a symbol of your relationship—perhaps a picture of your loved one, or a gift from that person—in front of you. Slowly repeat these words: "I, *(your name)*, now give you, *(other person)*, the power to make me whole. Without you, I am incomplete. You give me *(list your secondary gains here)* and satisfy my human needs for security, sensation, and power. I relinquish my power to you and will do whatever you ask in exchange for your

making me whole. If you try to move away, I will do whatever I can to get you to stay."

Now, introduce a *new* ritual, one designed to help you reclaim your personal power. Again, place the symbol of the person you love before you and say: "I, *(your name),* now reclaim my God-given gift of personal power from you, *(other person).* I now know that I have within me the ability to live a full, complete, and successful life; I now believe that what I need in life *(again, list secondary gains)* is there for me independent of our bond. I no longer need to try to overpower you. I let go of you easily and gently. I thank you for your attempt to make me whole while I was learning, growing, and claiming my birthright. And while I may choose to be with you as an enhancement to my life, my choice will spring from love, not from fear."

Which ritual felt right, and why?

Exploration Exercises:
Examining Your Personal Fears, Myths, and History

Once you've decided to reclaim your personal power and to relinquish pseudo-control over your partner, it is important to explore the complex roots of your addiction.

Often, we say we want one thing, yet we continue to work for another. That occurs because, on an unconscious level, what we have makes perfect sense to us. Therefore, it is crucial—and no simple task—to explore your own unconscious fears and myths, and to discover the personal reasons for your addictive relationships. Many addictive behaviors spring from forgotten or suppressed traumas that occurred during childhood or adolescence. Though such experiences may have been spirited away from our conscious minds, they greatly affect the decisions we make and the impressions we hold of the past.[2]

The following exercises are designed to launch you into self-discovery. Until we understand our own conscious and unconscious beliefs, we'll remain emotionally tied to habitual behaviors—even those we may want to change. It is one thing to try to *stop* a behavior; it is quite another to *understand* it. That requires discovery of how the behavior evolved.

Exercise 4-A: A Letter to the Self

One marvelous way to discover your unconscious beliefs is to write a letter to yourself.

Addictive love prevents true intimacy. If you are locked in an addictive relationship, some part of you fears intimacy. To dissipate that fear you must discover why it exists. Here is one way to help you do so.

1. Write a letter from the part of you that fears intimacy to the part of you that desires close, loving relationships. Let your fearful side tell
   A. why I, the fearful part, am here
   B. where I came from; what experiences, traumas, and lessons led to my fearful beliefs and behaviors
   C. how I perceive myself as a friend and protector
   D. what I fear
   E. what I need in order to willingly love in a truly intimate, vulnerable fashion
2. Now, write a letter from your fearful side that explains why you believe a supportive, intimate relationship eludes you. Tell the yearning side of yourself where you originated and how you've been choosing relationships in order to defend and support the belief that love isn't there for you.

Exercise 4-B: Learned Solutions

The next questions can help you study your social education and the role it plays in your current relationships.

1. Write down the most significant problem in your relationship.
2. Answer the following:
   A. If your mother had this same problem, how did she or how might she have solved it?
   B. If your father had this problem, how did he or how might he have solved it?
   C. Would their solutions be effective?
   D. Which parent are you most like?

Exercise 4-C: Learned Responses
In your imagination, create a scene in which the significant grown-ups in your life are gathered—a family reunion, a family celebration, etc. As a child, observe the grown-ups carefully. From your observations and intuition, what are you beginning to believe about love, relationships, power, men, and women? Complete the following statements based on what you experienced.

1. Love is _____

2. Relationships are _____

3. Women are _____

4. Men are _____

5. Relationships should _____

6. Power is _____

Examine your conclusions. Do they support healthy or addictive love? Have any of these beliefs come true in your adult relationships? How would you change any of these beliefs/conclusions to support healthy love?

Exercise 4-D: Coping with Relationship Problems
The following exercise can help you understand your own deeply held myths and beliefs.

Read through the entire exercise until you understand it. Relax by taking several deep breaths. Close your eyes and guide yourself through the exercise. Don't attempt to force images into your mind's eye; let them come to you at their own pace. Remember, images can be words, visions, feelings, or all three. (If you wish, you may enlist a friend to help guide you through the exercise.)

After you have imaged your responses, write them down. (If you have more than one bad feeling, take one at a time and repeat the exercise for each one.)

Think of the unpleasant feeling—anxiety, loneliness, fear, rejection, anger, boredom—you have experienced most often in your current relationship. Now, recall the most recent scene in which this feeling prevailed.

In your mind's eye, observe the scene as though you were observing it on a television screen. Who is there? What's happening and not happening? What's being said? What are you thinking or saying to yourself about yourself, others, and your life? As the scene unfolds, pay special attention to your negative thoughts. What is it you need in this scene that you aren't getting? How do you take care of yourself as it occurs?

Now, return to a time in your childhood (preferably early childhood—age six or under) when you experienced the same bad feeling. Let the scene appear on the TV screen. Again, don't force this scene into your mind; let it emerge gradually. If you have difficulty visualizing it, create a scene in which a parent or another significant adult is present. Observe the scene and become aware of details. Again, notice who is there, what is and isn't happening, and what's being said. Notice why you are experiencing the bad feeling. Are you taking care of that feeling? What do you want or need during this experience that you aren't getting? What are you doing to take care of yourself? What is your secret response to the scene as you are present in it? What do you begin to believe about yourself, others, and life based on what's going on there?

Now, carefully study the two scenes; scrutinize them for similarities. If, by magic, you could change the childhood scene so you felt better about yourself, others, and life, how might it be different? If the childhood scene *had* been different, how might the recent scene be different? Think about, then write down responses to, these questions.

Exercise 4-E: Rebirth

The following exercise—which may strike you as extraordinary—will help you explore your anxieties about separation and study their roots. Remember, patterns of belief and behavior begin very early; each life experience is recorded in the neurology of your body. This exercise takes that into account. Read through the exercise carefully until you understand it. Relax by taking several slow, deep breaths, then close your eyes and guide yourself through it.

Part I: Imagine you are observing the following on a screen. You are in the womb. Notice how it feels for you. Is it warm, carefree, safe, and secure? Notice how everything comes to you, and you need not do a thing. You are the center of your universe, and everything seems to revolve about you. You don't have to think or act; you simply exist. You are one with your mother. Experience yourself as floating and carefree. Linger with that good feeling. *Now* notice if there are any unpleasant or shocking experiences in the womb. Why are they happening?

Now, imagine your birth. Notice sudden changes. Perhaps the muscles around you are contracting. Perhaps your urge to be born is being resisted. Perhaps you experience pushing and pulling, anxiety, and pain. Take time to explore your feelings as they occur and as you emerge into the world.

Part II: Now you have emerged from the womb. Perhaps you feel anxious, sensing the strange new world of bright lights, cold hands, harsh voices, a slap on the bottom, separation from your mother, and a plunge into soapy water. How do you feel? Where did you feel safer—inside or outside the womb?

Part III: Follow yourself from birth to eighteen months of age. Take note of any traumas or fearful experiences such as extended periods of isolation, unresponsiveness to your needs, or sudden separation from your parents. Notice any anxiety you might have felt as one too young to make sense of what was happening. Carefully explore any anxious situations. Recall times in the recent past when you've experienced similar feelings. What connections are there between past and present? List beliefs and conclusions you may have drawn from these experiences.[3]

Exercise 4-F: Fear of Change
The paradox of personal change is that we have a strong urge to grow, yet we often fear and resist change. Make a list of all the reasons you might not want to change. Be honest!

Reprogramming Exercises:
Letting Go of the Old; Embracing the New

Listed here is the necessary process in moving from addiction to love.

1. Face the facts in your life and honestly examine your own role in your relationships.
2. Acknowledge resistance to change that stems from fear of not getting your secondary needs met.
3. Stop looking for "magic"—external solutions to your problems.
4. Look inward to examine fears, self-promises, and archaic beliefs that may support addictive beliefs and behaviors.
5. Reprogram the negative experiences.

To develop true openness to mature love, it is important to change the internal beliefs that hold you in dependent behavior. For lasting results in behavior change, internal inhibitions and false beliefs must be transformed from the inside out. As you try to learn why your current relationships make sense to your unconscious self and how to improve those relationships, keep in mind that you are the sum total of all your thoughts and experiences. Those thoughts and experiences produce results even when you're not aware of them. Therefore, when you gain some control over your internal "program," changes come easier and last longer. You should also understand that relinquishing an archaic belief might cause you great sadness and emotion. But that grief eventually will end, and the sadness will pass as the void is filled.

Exercise 5-A: Learning to Be Your Own Parent

What is self-parenting? It is the art of becoming a loving, forgiving mentor to yourself. Now that you've grown up, you have the ability to grant yourself those messages and pieces of information you may have missed in childhood and adolescence. This exercise is designed to guide you toward the wonderful independence that self-parenting provides.

Read carefully through the exercise. Take several deep breaths until you feel relaxed. Close your eyes and imagine you are a newborn baby. Feel your innocence and vulnerability; notice the naturalness of your body processes. Now, bring yourself as an adult into the scene and embrace the newborn you; hold the child close to your heart and slowly repeat the following: "Welcome; I'm so glad you're here. I've been waiting for you for a long time. I know how to take care of you, and what I don't know, I'm willing to learn. You can have what you need when you need it, and you can stop when you are full. All you need do is 'make noise' to let me know. I love you!"

Tell the infant (you) what it has a right to—a full, rich life—and what you plan to do to encourage that life. Take as much time as you need.

Tell the child (you) how you feel about child abuse; how you regret all the times you abused it or allowed others to abuse it. In particular, study any abuse you allowed in your love relationship. Again, take as much time as you need to fully feel any sorrow or regret. Remember, abuse can be emotional, mental, spiritual, or physical.

Tell the infant (you) that you're willing to provide it healthy love relationships from this moment on. And, before setting the inner child to rest, say you will always be there as a wise, loving parent, or that you will see to it that the child is in good hands. (Be specific about the kind of parenting you will provide or learn more about.)

Now, set the child to rest, knowing the child is *you* and will continue to reside within you. It is now your responsibility to acknowledge the child's needs. Remember, you have the potential to be a wise, protective, loving parent to yourself.

In the days after you do this exercise, you may want to enhance it by placing a picture of yourself as a baby or young child in a place where you will see it many times a day. Several times each day, affirm the child as part of you, and remind yourself that you are the parent, the problem solver. Take good care of yourself. Talk to the child within and tell it what it needs to hear to grow to self-love, autonomy, and intimacy.

Exercise 5-B: Your Future Relationships

This exercise helps you visualize future relationships. Read through it slowly and carefully. Take several deep breaths. Inhale, count to four slowly, exhale. Repeat five times. As you exhale, let go of discomfort and tension and allow yourself true relaxation—a prerequisite to vibrant imagination. The images you conjure may be visual images, word images, feeling images, or all of these.

If you've had difficulty with imagining exercises, keep in mind that people imagine in several ways—by listening, by seeing, and by feeling. Start with the style that is easiest for you. With time and practice, you'll soon find you can use all three modes of imagination.

Close your eyes. Imagine a television screen with a videocassette recorder. There are two tapes. The first tape begins to play. It is you five years from now without change in your relationships. The same problems that plague you now still exist. Take as much time as you need to let this image emerge into your mind's eye. Notice how you look; then pause. Notice how you feel about yourself, what you are thinking about yourself, others, and life. (Take time to fully explore each part of this.) Notice who is present in or absent from your life. Check your health; examine the feelings in and health of your heart, lungs, sexual organs, brain, stomach, blood vessels, and muscles. With things going wrong in your relationship, how does your body feel? What are you feeling or thinking as you review these images?

Now, leave that image and imagine that a second tape, one that shows a very different future scene begin to play. It is five years from now, and this time, things are different. Your life and relationships are characterized by harmony and happiness. You've changed the restrictive beliefs you formed in childhood and that once kept you from the love you so desired. Take as much time as you need to let this image emerge. Notice, again, how you look, how you feel, and what you think about yourself and others. What are you doing with your life? Who is there and who is not there? Explore your body again along with your health. How do you look and feel now that things are going well for you?

As you review this new image, what do you feel and think? The images in our minds and the energy in our bodies are closely linked.

The images we harbor—in or out of our awareness—contribute to our future reality. Most often, *what we think we are—we become.* If your relationship is troubled and addictive, you have thus far been acting out the first set of images. They have quietly affected your feelings, choices, and actions. Assuming you want the second set of images to take hold, it is essential that you embrace those images. Think about them several times a day until they are indelibly imprinted on your mind. From there they will be conveyed to every part of your being.

Carefully examine the second set of images. Define them as clearly as possible, allowing them to become more and more distinct each time you review them.

Now, choose a symbol from this second set of images, or create a new symbol, that will serve as a potent reminder of the future you want for yourself and your relationships. This should be a tangible object that you can view or use daily. Look at it often to remind yourself of the bright future you're working toward. Remember, the more you concentrate on positive images, the more quickly your old images will fade and the less power they will hold over your future.

Exercise 5-C: Finding the Spiritual Guide Within

This exercise is based on the premise that each of us contains a higher self characterized by love, wisdom, detachment, compassion, and spiritual intelligence. The spiritual guide within can be our greatest aid in solving life and relationship problems. Sadly, this higher level of consciousness is often subordinated to the lower instincts that give rise to our addictive tendencies. Real, mature love emanates from the higher self, and it is through our development of this spiritual guide that we will find enduring, sustaining love.

Read slowly through the fantasy that follows. Take several deep breaths until you feel relaxed. Inhaling through your nose and exhaling through your mouth, feel your innocence and vulnerability. Do this several times until your body fully relaxes and releases any distracting thoughts or tensions. Close your eyes.

When you feel ready, without hurrying yourself, imagine you are with a wise, caring, compassionate guide, spiritual teacher, or witness.

Ask the guide what you need to do to make your good images become future reality. Wait for the answer; if it is clear, thank the guide. If it isn't, continue communicating with the guide until the answer is clear. (Be sure the response comes from a wise, spiritual mentor and not a punitive, parental figure.) Thank the guide for direction and understanding, and know you can return for those things anytime you wish. Realize that this detached, compassionate guide is within you. Before you leave the guide, give it a gift—something that symbolizes what you're willing to give up to have the happy future relationship you so desire.

Exercise 5-D: Affirming the Positive
Most of you are familiar with the concept that positive thinking helps affect change. This idea is not new; it stems not only from modern psychology, but from ancient spiritual teachings that included the idea of prayer as creative visualization. The seeker is urged to avoid thoughts of failure and despair and to replace them with messages of faith, such as "All things are yours" (1 Cor. 3:21), and "As a man thinketh within himself, so is he" (Prov. 23:7).

On a scientific level, this positive process is described simply as action and reaction. An individual is the total of all his or her thoughts. Such thoughts determine action and affect results even when one is not conscious of them. The thoughts one radiates may be either positive or negative.

These exercises can help you realize that an understanding of unconscious beliefs and their resulting thoughts, images, choices, and behaviors is essential to positive change. Changing external behavior alone isn't enough; as we change negative internal "programs," external behavior follows suit in a surprising, wonderful way.

The following affirmation technique is a synthesis of ideas from many schools of positive thinking. It has worked well for me personally and for my clients. Let's define *affirmation* as a specific positive thought you create in response to a current need or goal.

We've heard negative programming thousands of times; now it is important to use our minds for positive results. Once we create a powerful positive affirmation, we must continue thinking it each day until it becomes a natural part of us. We can't erase the old and familiar, but we can create the new and have a choice in what we think or say to ourselves. At times the old and the new will come into conflict; this must be acknowledged and worked through.

Here is our affirmation exercise:

1. Define your desire (in this case, a relationship desire).
2. Think back to the parental message you needed as a child that could permit or affirm this desire.
3. Write the affirmation fifteen times, always including your name: five times in the first person, five times in the second, and five times in the third. (Example: "I, John, deserve love." "You, John, deserve love." "He, John, deserves love.")
4. Listen for any negative responses or feelings you experience while doing these affirmations; if there are any, write them down.
5. Continue to refine your affirmation so it fits comfortably against the negative responses. When it is as you want it, repeat it fifteen times.
6. Imagine your life as if the affirmation had become reality.
7. Release the thought; let your energy flow into pursuits that will turn it into reality.
8. Live your life as though the affirmation is reality. Create or respond to situations that can help you make your desire a reality.
9. Move through this exercise several times a day until the desire has become reality or the new belief feels natural to you, or both. You may switch from writing your affirmation to saying or thinking it.

Exercise 5-E: Impasse Dialogue

At times, the consciously chosen new message or affirmation will provoke the old, unconscious belief system, and a conflict will emerge. If this occurs, you experience a mental impasse or standoff. Often, a written dialogue between the two parts can help resolve the conflict. Repeat this dialogue until the two parts feel harmonious.

Exercise 5-F: Putting the Negative to Work for You

Addictive relationships are propped up by core beliefs within our Child Ego State that were born of emotionally painful experiences. As children, when we were upset, we told ourselves such things as, "Men (women) are dangerous"; "I'll never get what I need in life"; "People always hurt me"; "I'll never get close again." Such messages, formed in an emotional state, are automatically recorded in our neurology and become part of the foundation of our future reality. Addictive relationships allow us to repeat earlier life pains, and old emotions and myths will surface again and again. At such times, without realizing it, we tend to roll out the negative self-programs we gave ourselves as children. Thus, we often say, "I knew this would happen"; "This proves I should never love again"; "I'll never be this vulnerable again."

We programmed ourselves this way while we were in an emotional state. It makes sense that an opportune time for reprogramming ourselves for positive relationships may fall during periods of deep emotion. If you are struggling with an addictive relationship, you may well be feeling such emotion.

Moving from addiction to love means ending the cycle of repetitious self-history. It means reprogramming ourselves with messages that support healthy love relationships. Knowing about beliefs formed during profound states of emotion, *you can make use of your current pain—rather than fearing it—as an opportunity to prepare yourself for future healthy relationships.* When your heart is broken, you can tell yourself: "This pain will end and I will learn to love in healthier ways. I am determined to stop my destructive patterns of behavior because I deserve a healthier, happier love life."

Use your pain wisely. It can be your friend.

Though the following exercise may not be pleasant, since it involves concentration on pain or unhappiness you usually suppress, its use is certain to be followed by relief. Keep in mind, as you move through this exercise, that bringing bad feelings to the surface usually helps vanquish them.

1. Allow yourself to remember the pain that has troubled your relationship.

2. Listen carefully to negative core beliefs associated with that pain.
3. Even as you are conscious of your pain, say to yourself, "I now release myself from the old beliefs that have kept me mired in addictive love." (Think about all of the self-limiting beliefs you have become aware of.)
4. Give yourself a new message—an affirmation—that supports mature love. ("I will survive this pain and learn to love in healthy ways. I now know that love is there for me.")
5. Recognize that your pain has provided you with an opportunity for healing.
6. Trust that the pain eventually will go away. Let go!

Renewal Exercises: Moving Toward Mature Love

You've gained an understanding of how you've contributed to your tendency toward addictive love. You've explored your inner beliefs and begun to free yourself to love in wonderful new ways. You've learned that since you expect and demand less from love, you may get more from love.

When you give up self-limiting beliefs, you experience a high level of energy that brightens your outlook and your life. At this point, you are ready to let go of an unhealthy relationship to build on the strengths of one with the potential to be good.

Exercise 6-A: Forgiveness

I. Self-Forgiveness: While it is important that we become able to forgive others who have hurt us, we must also be willing to fully own up to the wounds of the heart that we have inflicted on others. Just as it is true that we can only love others to the degree we love ourselves, it is also true that we can only forgive others to the degree we can forgive ourselves. No one wants to admit that he or she has behaved as outrageously as others have toward him or her. Though we intended to love in good and noble ways, because of our own injuries or role models, we end up saying or doing things we later regret or deny. We often say or do things we promised ourselves that we would never, under any circumstances, say or do! And there we are, saying or doing them! Until we fully own up to such infractions, we continue to project them onto others. We all know how awful denial is.

We must be willing to go back in time and review our relationships and, with full honesty and accountability, be fair witness to our own abusive, hurtful, and injurious behaviors. Never mind whether we intended to do them or not. Never mind whether they were conscious or unconscious paybacks for injuries done to us. We must own and release each of these events and connect to the depth of regret or remorse that leads to healing. Regret and remorse come from the heart and soul, and can lead to the next step of forgiveness and healing, unlike self-blame, guilt, or shame, which are products of the ego. This process is internal, as distinct from confession, where the transaction is externally defined. Changes in our behavior occur when we fully acknowledge that we do not like what we have done because it goes against our own goodness, and when we feel the inner consequences of that acknowledgment.

Leaving denial can be the most healing step we take to attract healthier relationships into our lives. Done right, this exercise helps a person heal very deep heart wounds. Self-trust can be restored.

Read through the steps of the exercise. Create the time and space in which you can give this exercise full attention. Don't expect to get it done in one sitting. With full honesty, it may take hours, or days, to complete. Often, we see what is most obvious first. The subtle nuances generally appear later.

1. Relax physically with deep breathing. Clear your mind.
2. Take time to shift into your higher self, or witness, as described in exercise 5-C. Separate your witness from the self who hurt or betrayed others.
3. Let compassion emanate from your heart. Extend this feeling to the imperfect self.
4. Staying in your witness self, go back in time and recapture each hurtful experience. With honesty, acknowledge the ways you hurt others and the times you even enjoyed getting even.

5. Take one person at a time. Note how that person reacts to your hurtful behavior. As you are ready mentally, send love to the person.

6. Feel the regret and sorrow of each of your actions without self-blame. Observe and release the experience without judgment. Imagine the life energy trapped in that experience coming back to you.

7. Transform the experience by forgiving yourself. Trust that you have learned an important lesson. Note the freedom that you now feel.

8. Empower the experience by clarifying the lesson learned. Make a commitment to do what you can to stop the hurtful behaviors.

9. Make your amends to others as it feels right and as others are available to you. If you are not able to make amends to a person directly, visualize a dialogue between your higher self and his or her higher self. Or, write a letter that can later be burned or buried.

10. Feel gratitude for the lessons learned and the opportunity to grow. Acknowledge that we are all players in the game of life.

Now, you are ready to forgive others. You may even find it possible to forgive those who remain in denial and who continue to hurt you. As you forgive them, you may experience what seem like miracles as people you never dreamed would ever own their part of hurtful relationships come to you to make heartfelt amends.

II. Forgiveness of Others: One of the ways in which we cling to old, unhealthy ways is by harboring resentments, accusations, guilt, and anger. It is always best to let go of such feelings and try to forgive yourself and others for past mistakes and wrongs. When this comes with difficulty, which it often does, try to separate a persons actions from his or her personhood. Even if you can't accept people's actions, you may be able to forgive them. Learning to forgive is a process that necessarily involves the release of anger and resentment.

1. Make a list of the people you need to forgive; look particularly at past lovers.
2. As you review the list, pick out those people whom you still feel angry with. (Be honest; conning yourself may hurt future relationships.)
3. Write letters to each. Because you will not be sending them, you can fully express your anger. The anger does not have to be rational at this point because you already know that you, too, contributed to the situation that made you angry. Keep in mind that anger is a poison that separates you from others; you are expressing it in order to clear yourself for acceptance and forgiveness. It is nature's way to fill empty vessels; before we are free to say no to the expression of anger, we need to be free to say yes to it. Say yes for now.
4. Acknowledge that you cannot change what has happened in the past. Acknowledge that clinging to anger and resentment keeps you in an addictive cycle that excludes healthier love relationships. By letting go of old anger, you create a vacuum to be filled by new, better feelings.
5. Work to accept reality—what's happened has happened. Acceptance does not mean that you must like a person or his or her behavior. What lessons did you learn from the experience?
6. Now it is time to forgive. Take time out each day to sit quietly and forgive each person you've been out of harmony with in the past.
7. Make forgiveness a daily habit in your present relationships.

(*Note:* If you find you have difficulty forgiving a person, simply say, "I cannot humanly forgive this person, but my higher self will help me forgive and let go of resentment, for that is in my best interest.")

Exercise 6-B: A New Family Tree

As we give up addictive relationships, we acknowledge that one person cannot possibly meet all of our needs. Ideally, we are supported by a network of others, a large extended family. To assess your own network of support, you may want to create a new kind of family tree and see how many of its spots are filled for you.

1. Make a list of significant relatives and friends you have had or wanted to have.
2. Define the needs each fulfilled or the needs you wanted each to fulfill.
3. Evaluate your current situation to see how many of those people and roles are present.
4. Choose people in your present life who complement or fill those roles. (You can ask nonrelatives if they are willing to serve in the symbolic role of a sister, brother, etc.)
5. Work toward filling in your family tree and strengthening your network of support and love.

Exercise 6-C: Wellness Affirmation

To enter into and sustain a healthy love relationship, one must be complete in oneself and living a life of wellness. *Wellness,* in our context here, means knowing how to meet one's needs and not looking outside oneself for completeness.

Read slowly the following affirmations, personalizing them by inserting your name. If an affirmation feels out of sync, it is an indication that you may need to explore the disharmony, for it hints at a vulnerable spot in your relationship.

I, _____, now know what my real needs are and how to meet them.

I, _____, now am freely and effectively expressing my feelings to others.

I, _____, am acting assertively and in ways that consider the feelings and freedom of others.

I, _____, am enjoying my body by means of good nutrition, adequate exercise, and physical awareness.

I, _____, am engaged in activities that are meaningful to me and reflect my inner values.

I, _____, am creating and enjoying close, intimate relationships with others.

I, _____, am responding to challenges in life as opportunities for growth in strength and maturity.

I, _____, am creating the life I want rather than reacting to whatever happens.

I, _____, am using physical signals to bring into my life improvement and increased self-knowledge.

I, _____, am enjoying a sense of well-being even in times of adversity.

I, _____, know my own inner emotional and physical patterns and understand them to be signals from my inner self.

I, _____, trust my own personal resources as the greatest strength for living and growing.

I, _____, am experiencing myself as a wonderful person.

I, _____, am creating situations that help me realize my personal worth.

I, _____, believe there is abundance in life for me.

I, _____, am experiencing gratitude for life.

Exercise 6-D: Improving Your Relationship

When partners in a troubled relationship begin to work toward self-discovery, then make a commitment to their relationship, there are many things they can do immediately to help improve the relationship. These actions are closely linked to their new individual autonomy and self-esteem.

Remember, it is important to focus on the positive in yourself, others, and your life, and to build on what is already good in a love relationship. Of course, this does not mean problems should be dismissed. It means you and your partner can enhance what is good—and perhaps ease some problems—by letting each other know what is important to each of you. Listed here are some exercises to work on in your relationship.

1. *Do what you see lacking.* That is, rather than complaining about what your relationship lacks, work to fill the void and to communicate your values and desires to your partner. To truly work, this must be done without expectations; learn the joy of unconditional giving:
   A. If you feel ignored, acknowledge yourself and your partner.
   B. If you want a gift, give your partner something special.
   C. If you want a back rub, offer to give one.
   D. If you feel lonely, reach out to your partner and to others around you.
   E. If you want excitement, be exciting.
   F. If you want support, be supportive.
2. *Encourage your partner's growth.* Let your partner know all of the ways he or she encourages you and helps you grow. Express your appreciation for all of the good things your partner gives you. Ask your partner how you can be more helpful and supportive.
3. *Commit yourself to positive change.* Tell your partner how you're willing to change for the benefit of the relationship. (Be sure these changes spring from free choice, not from a forced promise. Free choice is experienced as voluntary yielding; a forced promise generates rebellion later.)
4. *Make use of rituals*—symbolic, repetitive actions that provide a sense of security and grounding to the child within each of us. Relationship rituals serve to affirm the importance of your bond. For example: a couple with jobs that involved travel wrote notes to each other to be opened on days they were apart. They found this ritual added meaning to the times they were separated.
   A. Think of a ritual that meant something to you as a child and adapt it to your adult life.
   B. Look at your current relationship. What rituals are developing? If they feel good, hang on to them.
   C. Work to create pleasant new rituals that help affirm your bond to your partner.

5. *Make giving special.* When you no longer expect and demand, the gifts and favors you are given have special value. Here's an exercise that has worked well for many couples.

    A. Make an uncensored list of all of the things you ever wanted from your partner. This list can cover all kinds of things, including sexual wishes.

    B. Exchange lists.

    C. Once a week, choose something from you partner's list and spontaneously give it to your partner.

6. *Create private time.* True intimacy blooms when individuals have uninterrupted time together to share feelings, thoughts, dreams, play, affection, and sex. A rule of thumb: an hour of sustained intimacy a day keeps troubles away!

7. *Serve each other.* When you commit yourself in true love, you agree to an almost spiritual yielding, to nourish your beloved, though occasionally it may mean you choose to postpone your own needs. Ask your partner, "How can I serve you?" The answer you receive will be much clearer than if you try to mind-read, as many people trapped in addictive relationships do. Distinguish between caretaking and caregiving.

8. *Nourish the relationship.* An emotionally healthy person is able to reach out to others, to embrace the good in others, and to let go of others when the time to let go comes. Work to develop the skills for living listed here.

    A. Express appreciation and thanks.

    B. Give spontaneously.

    C. Ask for what you need.

    D. Learn to listen.

    E. Be flexible.

    F. Accept disappointment and "no" from others; let go when you must.

    G. Resolve or manage conflicts as openly and with as little hostility as possible.

    H. Communicate honestly, from your center.

    I. Accept reality.
    J. Work to develop humility, objectivity, and a respect for life.

9. *Heart-to-Heart Bonding.* Though this is a profound and simple exercise, it is not easy for many partners to do. It is based on the premise that at the core of relationship problems is a violation of trust. The first developmental task we had to complete as children was to trust ourselves, others, and life.[4] When the heart is injured by a betrayal of that trust, we are reluctant ever after to share it fully, even though the more inspired part of us wishes to do so. Only by being willing to be vulnerable once again can we heal that betrayal. This is no easy task!

The following exercise has been suggested to partners wishing to renew their heartfelt bond after much hurt and betrayal of trust. I have been amazed at how many well-motivated individuals have resisted doing it. I have learned that if a couple is not willing to be emotionally vulnerable, there are limits to the amount of healing or emotional intimacy that can occur in their relationship. This exercise has also been suggested to couples working toward a sacred sexuality experience when recovering from a sexual addiction. In that regard, becoming comfortable sharing our hearts precedes sexual intimacy.

    A. Create a safe and nurturing environment that will allow for privacy and uninterrupted time. This should be mutually discussed and agreed upon.
    B. Position yourselves chest-to-chest in a way that allows each person to feel the best of the other's heart against his or her own.
    C. Breathe deeply and relax. Do not speak but instead share your love from the heart.
    D. Feel your partner's heartbeat. Stay with the experience.
    E. Observe any fear, distancing, or limiting thoughts without judgment. A broken heart takes time to heal and trust again.

F. Continue doing this exercise until it flows naturally and easily and there is a strong heartbeat exchange.

G. Now, share loving feelings heart-to-heart.

Expansion Exercise: Developing Personal Uniqueness

He who has a why to live can bear any how.

NIETZSCHE

Self-imposed limitations in your relationships not only sabotage those relationships, but keep you from achieving your individual potential. As you gain a sense of well-being, you contribute to the health of your relationships as well. And as your relationships provide you with a wonderful sense of interrelatedness with others, you are free to soar to new levels of awareness, meaning, and creativity you've never known before.

Life has but two directions—evolution and devolution; one is a forward motion, one a retrogression. Contrary to what many think, few people stand still; they are either on an upward or a downward spiral.

When faced with a problem we do not know how to solve, we continue to move in a downward spiral. Each time the problem recurs, our dilemma deepens. But if we work to resolve the problem, we spiral in a progressive, upward fashion. Though we may experience the same problem again later, we'll then examine it with greater understanding and confidence, and it will have less emotional impact.

As we give less control to our problems and more to ourselves, we find we're able to channel our energies in order to find our "place in the sun"—*not* as designed by our relationships, but as we really are. We each have something unique to contribute to the world, but sadly, because of the restrictions people place on themselves and others, such higher purpose often gets ignored or lost.

An addictive stance means that we look outward, denying and repressing the power of the self, and demand that life give us meaning. Once free of addictions, we realize life does not owe us anything; rather, it is our responsibility to give meaning to life. Freeing ourselves from past bonds does not guarantee a tension-free life, but it provides a healthy tension that challenges us to move toward an ideal of ourselves. The conquering of despair—the filling of what philosophers call the "existential void"—comes when we create our own lives, *mold* our own selves toward our ultimate potential, and contribute to the world community.

The exercises that follow may help you become more attuned to the higher level of consciousness from which your true purpose emanates. Remember that the higher self you seek to discover is more than the sum of its parts.

Exercise 7-A: The Personal Mission

Imagine yourself as a highly developed being somewhere in the cosmos, contemplating a voyage to planet Earth. You've been assigned to evaluate life on Earth and to use your knowledge and talents to enhance its quality. After much thought, you write out your goals:

My purpose on Earth will be _____

I'll accomplish this purpose by _____

I'll know I've succeeded when _____

Study your answers. What do they tell you about your deepest goals and dreams?

Exercise 7-B: Living Consciously

In addition to the opportunity to discover our ultimate purpose as human beings, life offers us situations that challenge us continually to make sense of it all. A person striving to live fully looks forward to all situations—even painful ones—as opportunities to expand into higher levels of consciousness.

The addictive person, on the other hand, does whatever he or she can to avoid difficult situations or to suppress problems or blame them on others in order to return to a false comfort as quickly and easily as possible. Addictions provide momentary relief; but conscious, fearless living provides true solutions to problems and long-term relief.

Listed here are some things to do to help you live more consciously.

1. Accept situations as they present themselves; don't shun or deny problems.
2. React to situations openly with your thoughts and feelings.
3. Take responsibility for whatever part you may have played in contributing to a problem.
4. Evaluate the truths such acknowledgment presents about yourself.
5. Study the choices you have.
6. Answer these questions: What lessons can I learn from this experience? How can I prevent this problem from recurring?

Exercise 7-C: Life Attitudes Learned

Complete these sentences as you believe your parents would have during your growing-up years. Give the first answer that comes to you.

Mother:

Life is _____

Life feels _____

Life should _____

Father:

Life is _____

Life feels _____

Life should _____

You:

Life is _____

Life feels _____

Life should _____

If the answers are negative, work to develop a positive life position.

Exercise 7-D: The Creative Universe Within

Do you imagine that the universe is agitated?
Go into the desert at night and look out at the stars.
This practice should answer the question.

HUA HU CHING[5]

We have learned that looking outside of oneself for happiness and fulfillment is what the ego was taught to do a long time ago, and what it tends to habitually do now. We are also learning that as we clear out our accumulated psychic glut and clutter, we discover an unlimited supply of creative energy within. The law of physics affirms that energy cannot be made to disappear, it can only be transformed.

To prevent a relapse into unhealthy relationships we are faced with the challenge of finding creative outlets for this generous gift of life energy. With renewed clarity we recognize that creative expression has been relegated to the backseat in our lives and in our society. Love and other addictions, both chemical and process, are the norm of the contemporary experience. We live in a culture that spends more money on promoting addictions; romantic fantasies; images of beauty, wealth, and fame; and sports gods and goddesses than it does on nourishing the heart and soul.

In the journey to healthy love, it is crucial that we unleash our passion in ways that acknowledge our creative urges and desire for wisdom. Embrace your vital energy and you will discover the seeds waiting to sprout and grow. All of your relationships will benefit as you calm down, stand still, and listen!

The following is a list of ideas for practices that may assist you in doing this. I promise, your efforts will be rewarded in significant ways.

1. contemplative praying
2. meditating
3. practicing body movement
4. practicing guided imagery
5. drumming
6. playing an instrument

7. listening to music
8. shamanic journeying
9. doing personal rituals
10. dancing
11. doing dreamwork
12. journal writing
13. inspirational reading
14. communing with nature
15. enjoying meaningful silence/solitude
16. gardening
17. creative cooking
18. creative writing
19. appreciating/making visual art
20. storytelling
21. stargazing
22. servicing others
23. appreciating/making creative art
24. playing
25. pondering the mystery of life

When practicing any of the above, maximize the experience by breathing deeply, clearing the mind, and being fully present.

Exercise 7-E: Daily Affirmation
As you begin each day, repeat this affirmation five times. As you repeat it, create an image of yourself as though this affirmation were a reality. "This is a time of divine fulfillment. The fruits of my labor and purpose of my life now unfold in clear, harmonious ways."

Best wishes on your journey toward self-discovery, self-affirmation, and true love. You have taken the time to get to know yourself and to improve the quality of your relationships and your life. You deserve love and life!

Notes

CHAPTER 1

1. Erich Fromm, *The Art of Loving* (New York: Harper and Row, 1962), 59–60.

2. Medieval writings, such as *The Art of Courtly Love*, by Andreas Capellanus, demonstrate how a balance of the feminine and masculine characterized the search for a mystical form of romantic love.

3. Ralph Waldo Emerson, *The Complete Writings of Ralph Waldo Emerson*, ed. Edward Emerson (New York: Wm. H. Wise and Co., 1929), 185.

4. Walt Whitman, *Leaves of Grass* (New York: Signet, 1958), 114. (Notes 3 and 4 are referenced in the article "The Poet of Body and Soul," by Mark Richard Barna, which appeared in the spring 1997 issue of *Gnosis: A Journal of the Western Inner Traditions*. The article addresses the struggle between license and repression of sexuality.)

5. Charlotte D. Kasl, *Women, Sex, and Addiction: The Search for Love and Power* (San Francisco: HarperSanFrancisco, 1990), 41.

6. In *Emotional Clearing*, by John Ruskin, and *The Sorcerers' Crossing*, by Taisha Abelar, there is an integration of spiritual practices and psychological clearing. Ruskin presents a self-help and meditation practice. Abelar focuses on the importance of recapitulation, the calling back of energy lost to past events in our lives.

7. Stanton Peele, with Archie Brodsky, *Love and Addiction* (New York: Signet, 1976).

8. *The Diagnostic and Statistical Manual of Mental Disorders*, third edition, revised (DSM-III-R), published by the American Psychological Association, 1987, lists nine criteria for the diagnosis of chemical dependency, at least three of which must be met for diagnosis. Most of the criteria concern behavior. In the DSM IV (APA, 1994), each mental disorder is conceptualized as a significant behavior, psychological syndrome, or pattern that results in distress or disability in an area of functioning, or in a significant increase in risk of suffering pain, death, disability, or an important loss of freedom. The descriptive terms *love addiction, romance addition,* and *sexual addiction* do not appear in DSM-IV. These are subsumed in various diagnostic categories, and a complete and comprehensive assessment is

necessary. Also, it is possible for a single disorder to fit more than one diagnostic category. In my experience working with people attached to love objects in unhealthy or destructive ways, it is not uncommon to have a diagnosis of depression or anxiety; a personality disorder and physical illness, and substantial relational, financial, or other problems that are interfering with treatment and overall functioning. A. Goodman, in his list of criteria for an addictive disorder (1990) suggests that any behavior that is used to produce gratification and to escape internal discomfort can be engaged in compulsively and can constitute an addictive disorder. Jennifer P. Schneider, in an article in the journal *Sexual Addiction & Compulsivity* (vol. 1, no. 1 [1994]: 19–45, summarized the key elements of any addictive disorder as loss of control, continuation despite adverse consequences, and a preoccupation of obsession. (See also Schneider and Irons, *Sexual Addiction & Compulsivity* vol. 3, no. 1 [1997]: 7–9).

9.   Harvey Milkman and Stanley Sunderwirth, *Craving for Ecstasy: The Consciousness and Chemistry of Escape* (Lexington, Mass.: Lexington Books, 1987).

10.   Helen E. Fisher, *Anatomy of Love: The Natural History of Monogamy, Adultery, and Divorce* (New York: Fawcett Columbine, 1992), 57.

11.   Dorothy Tennov, in her book *Love and Limerance: The Experience of Being in Love* (New York: Stein and Day, 1979), described limerance as being a romantically compelled high.

12.   Milkman and Sunderwirth, 45.

13.   Mark Laaser, in *The Secret Sin* (Grand Rapids, Mich.: Zondervan, 1992), states that experts in the field of sexual addiction speculate that as much as 10 percent of the Christian population is sexually addicted and that it is time to address the problem so that true spiritual healing can occur.

14.   Patrick Carnes, *Don't Call It Love; Recovery from Sexual Addiction* (New York: Bantam, 1991). This classic book describes various aspects of sexual addiction and the recovery process. It is based on the stories of 1,000 people and their families afflicted with the disease and committed to recovery.

15.   In his book *Silently Seduced: When Parents Make Their Children Partners— Understanding Covert Incest* (Deerfield Beach, Fla.: Health Communications, 1991), Kenneth Adams presents an understanding of covert incest. He limits his scope to opposite-sex incest survivors while acknowledging that same-sex covert incest damage is parallel.

CHAPTER 2

1.   Helen E. Fisher, in her book *The Sex Contract* (New York: William Morrow and Co., 1983), gives an anthropological perspective of how the changing of the female estrous cycle affected human relationships.

2.   Patrick Carnes, *Don't Call It Love; Recovery from Sexual Addiction* (New York: Bantam, 1991), 31–32.

3. Michael Liebowitz, *The Chemistry of Love* (Boston: Little, Brown, 1983).

4. Brenda Schaeffer, *Loving Me, Loving You: Balancing Love and Power in a Codependent World* (San Francisco: Harper Collins, 1992), 47.

5. Riane Eisler, *Sacred Pleasure: Sex, Myth, and the Politics of the Body—New Paths to Love and Power* (San Francisco: HarperSanFrancisco, 1995), 244–45.

6. These quotes were taken from both local and national nightly newscasts of the major broadcasting companies as viewed in the Minneapolis–St. Paul, Minnesota, area.

7. Pia Mellody, in *Facing Love Addiction: Giving Yourself the Power to Change the Way You Love—The Love Connection to Codependence* (San Francisco: HarperSanFrancisco, 1992), 49, distinguishes love addicts and love avoidance addicts. My premise is that both love addiction and love avoidance are incorporated in the psyche of the love addict.

8. Abraham Maslow, *Toward a Psychology of Being* (Princeton, N.J.: Van Nostrand Reinhold, 1968) and *The Farther Reaches of Human Nature* (New York: Viking, 1971).

9. Jacquelyn Small, *Transformers: The Artist of Self-Creation* (New York: Bantam, 1992), 2, 193.

CHAPTER 3

1. Several transactional analysis references are utilized in this chapter: Eric Berne, *What Do You Say After You Say Hello?* (New York: Grove Press, 1972) and *Games People Play* (New York: Grove Press, 1964); Muriel James and Dorothy Jongeward, *Born to Win: Transactional Analysis with Gestalt Experiments* (Redding, Mass.: Addison-Wesley, 1996); Michael Brown and Stanley Woollams, *Transactional Analysis: A Modern and Comprehensive Text of TA Theory and Practice* (Dexter, Mich.: Huron Valley Institute, 1978); Claude Steiner, *Scripts People Live Transactional Analysis of Life Scripts* (New York: Grove Press, 1974). Transactional analysis theory takes complex psychological information and presents it in clear, comprehensible language that empowers the client. It has been criticized for the simplicity of its language and its reliance on jargon.

2. The author's *Corrective Parenting Chart* is a summary of the developmental stages, needs, and tasks of each stage; parental dos and don'ts; problems that occur in childhood and adulthood when needs/tasks are not met; and corrective measures that can be taken. It is an integration of ideas from the developmental theories of Freud, Erickson, Piaget, and Berne. The chart is available from the author (see page 195).

CHAPTER 4

1. Psychological needs going unmet in relationships can result in suicide, homicide, AIDS, as well as anxiety, depression, despair, and a host of physical illnesses.

2. More on boundaries and the characteristics of healthy love can be found in chapter 8 of the author's *Loving Me, Loving You* (Center City, Minn: Hazelden, 1991).

3. Stanley Woollams and Michael Brown, *Transactional Analysis: A Modern and Comprehensive Text of TA Theory and Practice* (Dexter, Mich.: Huron Valley Institute Press, 1978), 84–92.

4. Woollams and Brown, *Transactional Analysis*, 134–37.

CHAPTER 5

1. Chapter 5 in the author's *Loving Me, Loving You* gives an in-depth discussion on the problem of experiencing power as a commodity. Chapter 2 of that book addresses power bases as they are culturally assigned to men and women and how they tend to lock us in power struggles.

CHAPTER 6

1. Kahlil Gibran, *The Prophet* (New York: Random House, 1951).

2. Erich Fromm, *The Art of Loving* (New York: Harper and Row), 53.

3. Brenda Schaeffer, *Loving Me, Loving You: Balancing Love and Power in a Codependent World* (San Francisco: Harper Collins, 1992), 158–59.

4. Richard Bach, *The Bridge Across Forever* (New York: William Morrow and Co., 1984) 210.

5. Claude Steiner, handout at conference.

6. Schaeffer, *Loving Me, Loving You*, 170–71.

7. Eric Berne, *What Do You Say After You Say Hello?* 137–39. Rackets are now thought to be a composite of distorted feelings supported by internal beliefs and expressed in external behaviors, as described by Richard Erskine and Marilyn Zalcman in "Rackets and Other Treatment Issues," *Transactional Analysis Journal* 9, no. 1 (January 1979).

8. Schaeffer, *Loving Me, Loving You*, 193–94.

9. Bach, *The Bridge Across Forever*, 286.

CHAPTER 7

1. Norman Cousins, *Human Options* (New York, London: W.W. Norton and Co., 1981), 34.

2. Margery Williams, *The Velveteen Rabbit* (New York: Doubleday and Co., 1975), 16–17.

3. Viktor E. Frankl, *Man's Search for Meaning* (New York: Pocket Books, 1963), 58–60.

4. C. Norman Shealy, *90 Days to Self-Health* (New York, Bantam Books, 1978), 36, 45. Our central management system, the hypothalamus and the limbic systems, seems to require that habits be patterned and repeatedly programmed to reach the lower levels of consciousness.

5. A. Guillaumont, H.-CH. Puech, and G. Quipel, trans., *The Gospel According to Thomas* (New York: Harper and Row, 1959), Logian 45.

CHAPTER 8

1. The self-help exercises offered here were developed by the author for specific workshop modules and in response to client requests and needs. They have been modified for a reading audience, though some may wish to record the exercises on audiocassette tape for greater ease of use. Do as much or as little of each exercise as is comfortable, and seek professional help when needed.

2. What you *think* may have happened in the past, and your impressions, conclusions, and beliefs about past events, are at least as important as what, in fact, occurred. Past events cannot be changed; sometimes, they cannot even be corroborated. However, how we feel about those events, how we interpret and frame them in our lives, *can* be changed.

3. Charles L. Whitfield's *Memory and Abuse: Remembering and Healing the Wounds of Trauma* (Deerfield Beach, Fla.: Health Communications, 1995) is a thoroughly documented, groundbreaking work on healing from the effects of childhood trauma. It addresses the psychology of memory, the history of child abuse, ways to verify and corroborate a memory, and methods for sorting true from untrue memories.

4. Erik Erickson, a pioneer in child-development theory, stresses that learning to trust the self, others, and life is the first and fundamental task we must each complete. It is the critical building block for later stages of development. Translated into our adult relationships, it becomes the foundation of a feeling of safety.

5. Brian Walker, *Hua Hu Ching: The Unknown Teachings of Lao Tzu* (San Francisco: HarperSanFrancisco, 1995), 7.

Bibliography

Abelar, Taisha. *The Sorcerers' Crossing: A Woman's Journey.* New York: Penguin Books, 1983.

Adams, Kenneth M. *Silently Seduced: When Parents Make Their Children Partners—Understanding Covert Incest.* Deerfield Beach, Fla.: Health Communications, 1991.

Bach, Richard. *The Bridge Across Forever: A True Love Story.* New York: William Morrow and Co., 1984.

Beattie, Melody. *Beyond Codependency: And Getting Better All the Time.* Center City, Minn.: Hazelden, 1989.

Berne, Eric. *Transactional Analysis in Psychotherapy: A Systematic Individual and Social Psychiatry.* New York: Grove Press, 1961.

———. *Games People Play.* New York: Grove Press, 1964.

———. *What Do You Say After You Say Hello?* New York: Grove Press, 1972.

Bly, Robert. *Iron John: A Book about Men.* Reading, Mass.: Addison-Wesley, 1990.

Branden, Nathaniel. *The Psychology of Romantic Love.* Toronto: Bantam Books, 1980.

Buscaglia, Leo. *Love.* New York: Fawcett Crest, 1972.

Campbell, Joseph, with Bill Moyers. *The Power of Myth.* New York: Doubleday, 1988.

Capellanus, Andreas. *The Art of Courtly Love.* Edited by Frederick W. Locke. New York: Ungar, 1957.

Capra, Fritjof. *The Turning Point.* New York: Bantam Books, 1983

———. *Uncommon Wisdom.* New York: Bantam Books, 1989.

Carnes, Patrick, editor. "Sexual Addiction and Compulsivity," *The Journal of Treatment and Presentations* vol. 1, no. 1 (1994).

———. *Contrary to Love: Helping the Sexual Addict.* Minneapolis, Minn.: CompCare, 1989.

———. *Don't Call It Love: Recovery from Sexual Addiction.* New York: Bantam Books, 1991.

———. *Out of the Shadows: Understanding Sexual Addiction.* Minneapolis, Minn.: CompCare, 1983.

———. *Sexual Anorexia: Overcoming Sexual Self-Hatred.* Center City, Minn.: Hazelden, 1997.

Clarke, Jean Illsley. *Self-Esteem: A Family Affair.* San Francisco: Harper-SanFrancisco, 1985.

Colgrove, Melba, Harold H. Bloomfield, and Peter McWilliams. *How to Survive the Loss of a Love.* Toronto: Bantam Books, 1976.

Cousins, Norman. *Human Options: An Autobiographical Notebook.* New York, London: W.W. Norton and Co., 1981.

Covington, Stephanie. *Leaving the Enchanted Forest: The Path from Relationship Addiction.* San Francisco: HarperSanFrancisco, 1988.

DeMause, L., "The Universality of Incest," *Journal of Psychohistory* vol. 19, no. 2: 123–64.

Diamond, Jed. *Looking for Love in All the Wrong Places: Overcoming Romantic and Sexual Addictions.* New York: Avon, 1988 and 1989.

Eisler, Riane. *The Chalice and the Blade: Our History, Our Future.* San Francisco: HarperSanFrancisco, 1988.

———. *Sacred Pleasure: Sex, Myth, and the Politics of the Body—New Paths to Power and Love.* San Francisco: HarperSanFrancisco, 1996.

Fisher, Helen E. *The Sex Contract.* New York: William Morrow and Co., 1982.

———. *Anatomy of Love: The Mysteries of Mating, Marriage, and Why We Stray.* New York: Fawcett Columbine, 1993.

Fox, Matthew. *Original Blessing.* Santa Fe: Bear and Co., 1983.

Frankl, Viktor E. *Man's Search for Meaning.* New York: Pocket Books, 1963.

Freud, Sigmund. *Sexuality and the Psychology of Love.* New York: Collier Books, 1963.

Fromm, Erich. *The Art of Loving.* New York: Harper and Row, 1962.

Gibran, Kahlil. *The Prophet.* New York: Random House, 1951.

Goulding, Robert, and Mary McClure Goulding. *Changing Lives Through Redecision Therapy.* New York: Brunner/Mazel, 1979.

———. *The Power Is in the Patient.* San Francisco: TA Press, 1978.

Grof, Christina, and Stanislav Grof. *The Stormy Search for the Self: A Guide to Personal Growth through Transformational Crisis.* Los Angeles: Tarcher, 1990.

Grubbman-Black, Stephen D. *Broken Boys/Mending Men.* New York: Ivy Books, 1990.

Hunter, Mic. *Abused Boys: The Neglected Victims of Sexual Abuse.* New York: Fawcett Columbine, 1990.

Ingerman, Sandra. *Soul Retrieval: Mending the Fragmented Self through Shamanic Practice.* San Francisco: HarperSanFrancisco, 1991.

James, Muriel and Dorothy Jongeward. *Born to Win.* Redding, Mass.: Addison-Wesley, 1991.

Johnson, Robert A. *He: Understanding Masculine Psychology.* New York: Harper and Row, 1986.

———. *Inner Work: Using Dreams and Creative Imagination.* San Francisco: Harper and Row, 1986.

————. *She: Understanding Feminine Psychology*. New York: Harper & Row, 1997.

————. *We: Understanding the Psychology of Romantic Love*. San Francisco: Harper & Row, 1983.

Kasl, Charlotte D. *Women, Sex, and Addiction: The Search for Love and Power*. San Francisco: HarperSanFrancisco, 1990.

Keyes, Ken, Jr. *Handbook to Higher Consciousness*. Berkeley: Love Lines Books, 1975.

————. *A Conscious Person's Guide to Relationships*. Coos Bay, Oreg.: Love Line Books, 1979.

Laaser, Mark R. *Faithful and True: Sexual Integrity in a Fallen World*. Grand Rapids, Mich.: Zondervan, 1996.

Labowitz, Robbi Shoni. *Miraculous Living*. New York: Simon and Schuster, 1996.

Lerner, Harriet. *The Dance of Intimacy: A Woman's Guide to Courageous Acts of Change in Key Relationships*. New York: Harper Perennial, 1990.

Mellody, Pia. *Facing Love Addiction: Giving Yourself the Power to Change the Way You Love*. San Francisco: HarperSanFrancisco, 1992.

Palmer, Helen. *The Enneagram: Understanding Yourself and Others in Your Life*. New York: Harper and Row, 1988.

————. *The Enneagram in Love and Work: Understanding Your Intimate and Business Relationships*. San Francisco: Harper and Row, 1995.

Peck, M. Scott. *The Road Less Traveled*. New York: Simon and Schuster, 1978.

Peele, Stanton, with Archie Brodsky. *Love and Addiction*. New York: Signet, 1976.

Phillips, Robert D. *Structural Symbiotic Systems*. Author, 1975.

Ponder, Catherine. *The Dynamic Laws of Prosperity*. Englewood Cliffs, N.J.: Prentice Hall, 1962.

Ray, Sondra. *I Deserve Love: How Affirmations Can Guide You to Personal Fulfillment*. Millbrae, Calif.: Les Femmes, 1976.

————. *Loving Relationships*. Berkeley: Celestial Arts, 1980.

Ruskan, John. *Emotional Clearing: A Self-Therapy Guide to Releasing Negative Feelings*. New York: R. Wyler and Co., 1993.

Schaef, Anne Wilson. *When Society Becomes an Addict*. San Francisco: Harper and Row, 1987.

————. *Escape from Intimacy, Untangling the "Love Addictions": Sex, Romance and Relationships*. San Francisco: HarperSanFrancisco, 1990.

Schaeffer, Brenda. *Corrective Parenting Chart*. Author, 1979.

————. *Corrective Parenting Chart*. 4th ed. Author, 1993.

————. *Loving Me, Loving You: Balancing Love and Power in a Codependent World*. Center City, Minn: Hazelden, 1991..

Scheid, Robert. *Beyond the Love Game: An Inner Guide to Finding Your Mate*. Millbrae, Calif.: Celestial Arts, 1980.

Schneider, Jennifer P. *Back from Betrayal: Recovering from His Affairs*. Center City, Minn.: Hazelden, 1988.

Schneider, Jennifer P., and Bert Schneider. *Sex, Lies and Forgiveness: Couples Speaking Out on Healing from Sex Addiction.* Center City, Minn.: Hazelden, 1991.

Shealy, C. Norman. *90 Days to Self-Health.* New York: Bantam, 1978.

Sipes, A.W. Richard. *Sex, Priests, and Power.* New York: Brunner/Mazel, 1995.

Small, Jacquelyn. *Transformers: The Artists of Self-Creation.* New York: Bantam, 1992.

Steiner, Claude. *Scripts People Live: Transactional Analysis of Life Scripts.* New York: Grove Press, 1974.

Weed, Joseph. *Wisdom of the Mystic Masters.* West Nyack, N.Y.: Parker Publishing Co., 1968.

Weiss, Laurie, and Jonathan Weiss. *Recovery from Co-Dependency: It's Never Too Late to Reclaim Your Childhood.* Deerfield Beach, Fla.: Health Communications, 1989.

Whitfield, Charles L. *Memory and Abuse.* Deerfield Beach, Fla.: Health Communications, 1995.

Williams, Margery. *The Velveteen Rabbit.* New York: Doubleday and Co., 1975.

Woollams, Stanley, and Michael Brown. *Transactional Analysis: A Modern and Comprehensive Text of TA Theory and Practice.* Dexter, Mich.: Huron Valley Institute Press, 1978.

Woollams, Stanley, Michael Brown, and Kristyn Huige. *Transactional Analysis in Brief.* Ypsilanti, Mich.: Spectrum Psychological Services, 1974.

Resources for Further Information

National Council for Sexual
   Addiction and Compulsivity
   (NCSAC)
1090 Northchase Parkway South,
   Suite 200
Marietta, GA 30067
770/989-9754
ncsac@telesystem.com
www.ncsac.org

Sex Addicts Anonymous (SAA)
P.O. Box 3038
Minneapolis, MN 55403
713/869-4902 or 213/896-2964
   in Los Angeles, CA

Sex and Love Addicts Anonymous
   (SLAA)
P.O. Box 650010, 437 Cherry Street
West Newton, MA 02165-0010
617/332-1845

Co-Sex Addicts Anonymous
9337-B
Katy Freeway
Houston, TX 77042

Sexaholics Anonymous (SA)
P.O. Box 111910
Nashville, TN 37222-1910
615/331-6230

Sexual Compulsives Anonymous
   (SCA)
P.O. Box 1585 Old Chelsea Station
New York, NY 10011
212/439-1123 or 310/859-5585

Recovering Couples Anonymous
   (RCA)
P.O. Box 11872
St. Louis, MO 63105
314/830-2600

National Council for Couple and
   Family Recovery (NCCFR)
(Jim and Mary Lane)
434 Lee Avenue
St. Louis, MO 63119
314/963-8898

Index

How to Contact the Author

BRENDA M. SCHAEFFER, M.A., is a licensed psychologist, a certified addiction specialist, and an experienced psychotherapist, trainer, and communications consultant. In addition, she is a national and international lecturer and workshop presenter. She unites a wide range of topics in her repertoire of presentations, and brings Western psychology and various world philosophies into her work. She believes that painful life events are wake-up calls and that therapy should be movement forward on a soul's journey.

Brenda has served on the board of directors of the National Council of Sexual Addictions and Compulsivity; is a member of the International Transactional Analysis Association and the International Association of Enneagram Teachers; and is clinical director of Healthy Relationships, Inc. Her other publications include *Loving Me, Loving You: Balancing Love and Power in a Co-dependent World*; *Signs of Healthy Love*; *Signs of Addictive Love*; *Power Plays*; and *Addictive Love: Help Yourself Out*. *Is It Love or Is It Addiction?* has been translated into Spanish and German.

If you are interested in contacting Brenda for speaking engagements, workshops, or consults, or if you'd like to be on her mailing list, you may write, e-mail, or call her at

Brenda M. Schaeffer
Healthy Relationships, Inc.
P.O. Box 844
Chanhassen, MN 55317

e-mail: brenda@spacestar.net
World Wide Web site: http://www.loveandaddiction.com
1-888-987-6129 (toll free)